# HEADWAY

## INTERMEDIATE
## PRONUNCIATION

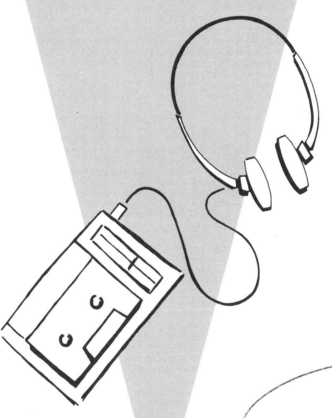

## Sarah Cunningham    Bill Bowler

### Oxford University Press

Oxford University Press
Walton Street, Oxford OX2 6DP

Oxford New York
Athens Auckland Bangkok Bombay
Calcutta Cape Town Dar es Salaam Delhi
Florence Hong Kong Istanbul Karachi
Kuala Lumpur Madras Madrid Melbourne
Mexico City Nairobi Paris Singapore
Taipei Tokyo Toronto

and associated companies in
Berlin Ibadan

OXFORD and OXFORD ENGLISH are trade
marks of Oxford University Press

ISBN 0 19 433968 8

© Oxford University Press, 1990

First published 1990
Fourth impression 1994

The authors would like to acknowledge the
writers of various standard pronunciation
reference books, especially Ann Baker
*Introducing English Pronunciation*, A. C.
Gimson *A Practical Course of English
Pronunciation*, Joanne Kenworthy
*Teaching English Pronunciation*, Colin
Mortimer *Elements of Pronunciation*, and
P. Roach *English Phonetics and
Phonology*. We would especially like to
express our whole-hearted thanks to John
and Liz Soars for their careful reading of
the manuscript, and their invaluable
criticism, advice, and constant
encouragement. We would also like to
thank the people at Oxford University
Press for their tireless help and unbounded
enthusiasm.

Cartoon illustrations by Nigel Paige.

The publishers and authors would like to
thank the Times Newspapers Limited for
their kind permission to use an extract
from 'How Ruth made history at Oxford',
by Isabel Hilton, first published in 1982.
© Times Newspapers Ltd. 1987.

Designed by Holdsworth Associates
Set by Pentacor PLC
Printed in Hong Kong

# CONTENTS

* These exercises require reference to *Headway Intermediate Student's Book*, page numbers of which are given. All other exercises can be done without reference to the Student's Book.

# UNIT 3

# UNIT 4

# UNIT 11

## ● Sounds

## ● Connected speech

## ● Intonation and sentence stress

## ● Word focus

## ● Everyday English

# UNIT 12

## ● Sounds

## ● Connected speech

## ● Intonation

## ● Word focus

## ● Everyday English

# INTRODUCTION

This book is intended for intermediate level students who wish to improve their pronunciation and, at the same time, practise the new grammar and vocabulary that they have been studying. It is designed as part of the *Headway* course and each of the fourteen units in this book is closely linked to the fourteen corresponding units of *Headway Intermediate*. However, most of the material in *Headway Pronunciation* could easily be used by intermediate students following other courses. The exercises are suitable either for classroom use or for students working independently.

## ● Syllabus

All the main pronunciation problems of foreign learners are covered in this book, in five sections:

1   **Sounds**  These exercises look at individual sounds or groups of sounds that cause problems to speakers of particular languages. These languages are indicated in the exercises as follows:

(D) German   (Gr) Greek      (J) Japanese

(E) Spanish   (H) Hungarian   (P) Portuguese

(F) French    (I) Italian     (Tr) Turkish

The exercises include diagrams showing how the sounds are made correctly.

2   **Connected speech**  These exercises look at the way that the pronunciation of individual words can change when they are part of a phrase or sentence. In particular, they deal with weak and strong forms, and word linking.

3   **Intonation (and sentence stress)**  These exercises look at the most common intonation patterns and problems in English. They train students to hear different types of intonation and provide practice in some of the most common areas where problems occur; for example, making polite requests, showing interest, disagreeing politely, and so on.

4   **Word focus**  These exercises look at groups of words where there are problems with sounds and word stress. Usually these are Latin-based words with problematic prefixes and suffixes, but there are also lexical sets.

5   **Everyday English**  These exercises look at areas where meaning is normally internationally understood, but where pronunciation is often difficult; for example, saying the names of countries, saying fractions or saying temperatures.

In each unit there are exercises on each of these five areas.

## ● Integration with the *Headway* course

As well as providing a systematic pronunciation syllabus, the exercises in *Headway Pronunciation* aim to extend and consolidate the work done in the main *Headway* coursebook. Wherever possible they relate to the grammar and vocabulary introduced in the Student's Book, providing the opportunity for either further practice or revision. Often they make use of the Reading and Listening texts that appear in the Student's Book. The link with the main course material is indicated in the Contents Pages of this book.

## ● Using *Headway Pronunciation*

The exercises in this book can be used in a number of ways. All are suitable for use in class, and some include pairwork and groupwork. However, almost all of the exercises can be used equally by the student working independently – in a language laboratory, in a self-access centre, or at home. Those exercises ideally to be used in a language laboratory are indicated with the following symbol: ∩

## ● Tapes

*Headway Pronunciation* is accompanied by three tapes, which provide all the necessary models and practice material. The tape material for each exercise is often divided into sections (**A, B, C,** etc.). The following type of symbol in the exercise indicates exactly which tape material is to be used:

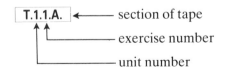

If the words that occur on the tape are not given exactly in the exercise then the tapescript is provided in the key at the back of the book.

## ● Key

As in the rest of the *Headway* course, the student is encouraged to work out rules for him or herself, through directed questions. The answers to these questions are provided in the key at the back of the book. The key also provides the necessary answers to exercises, as well as tapescripts not given in the exercise itself. Entries in the key are indicated with this symbol: ⊶

## ● The phonemic alphabet

The phonemic symbols used in this book are the ones used in all Oxford Dictionaries. More or less the same symbols are used in most other modern dictionaries and coursebooks too. Because English pronunciation/spelling rules are so irregular, it is very important for students to know the phonemic alphabet if they want to use dictionaries independently, outside the classroom. It is also essential for students to be familiar with the symbols if they want to use this book properly. An extra unit is therefore included at the beginning of the book, designed to teach the phonemic alphabet. There are also regular transcription exercises in the Word focus exercises, to practise reading the phonemic script.

## ● Terminology

Many students will not be familiar with the basic terminology of phonetics. Below is a list of terms used in this book, together with examples. Use these pages as a reference while you are using the book.

| | |
|---|---|
| **Vowels** | There are five vowels in English – *a, e, i, o,* and *u.* |
| **Vowel sounds** | There are **twelve** vowel sounds in English represented by the phonemic symbols / iː /, / ɪ /, / ʊ /, / uː /, / e /, / ə /, / ɜː /, / ɔː /, / ɒ /, / ʌ /, / æ /, and / ɑː /. |
| **Diphthongs** | There are eight diphthongs in English – / aɪ /, / aʊ /, / eɪ /, / eə /, / ɪə /, / əʊ /, / ʊə /, and / ɔɪ /. They are made from two vowel sounds put together. The first sound is longer than the second sound. |
| **Schwa** | The sound / ə / as in *the* / ðə /. This is the most common vowel sound in English. It is **never** stressed and is often found in weak forms. |
| **Consonants** | The letters of the alphabet that are not vowels – *b, c, d, f, g, h, j, k, l, m, n, p, q, r, s, t, v, w, x, y,* and *z.* |
| **Consonant sounds** | The sounds made by the letters above. In the phonemic alphabet there are these additional symbols / θ /, / ð /, / ʃ /, / ʒ /, / tʃ /, / dʒ /, and / ŋ /. *c, q, x,* and *y* are **not** phonemic symbols. |

| | |
|---|---|
| **Voiced sounds** | Sounds where the voice is needed to make the sound. All vowels and diphthongs are voiced, and so are the following consonant sounds: / b /, / v /, / ð /, / d /, / z /, / ʒ /, / dʒ /, / g /, / m /, / n /, / ŋ /, / w /, / j /, / l /, and / r /. |
| **Voiceless sounds** | Sounds where the voice is **not** needed to make the sounds: / p /, / h /, / f /, / θ /, / t /, / s /, / ʃ /, / tʃ /, and / k /. |
| **Weak and strong forms** | Many auxiliary verbs (like *are, was, have, can* etc.), prepositions (like *at, for, from, to* etc.), pronouns and possessives (like *you* and *your*) have two different pronunciations. In the **strong form** the vowel is fully pronounced. In the **weak form** it is shortened so that we can say the word more quickly. Often the vowel in the weak form is a *schwa* ( / ə / ) sound. |

| Example | Weak form | Strong form |
|---|---|---|
| *have* | *Have* / həv / you been home? | Yes, I *have.* / hæv / |
| *at* | He isn't *at* / ət / home. | What are you looking *at*? / æt / |
| *your* | Can I borrow *your* / jə / pen? | That's not *your* / jɔː / pen, it's mine. |

| | |
|---|---|
| **Word stress** | The strongest syllable in a word is the syllable with the **stress** on it. All words have a stressed syllable when you say them individually, but we do **not** mark the stress in one-syllable words. In this book word stress is marked like this: |

● syllable

In dictionaries it is marked like this:

'syllable

| | |
|---|---|
| **Sentence stress** | In the same way, some syllables in the sentence are stronger than others. In a sentence, the stressed syllables are in the words that give the main message of the sentence, usually **nouns, verbs,** and **adjectives.** In this book, sentence stress is marked with boxes like this: |

☐ ☐ ☐ ☐
Karen has broken her new glasses.

**Main stress in sentences**

In any phrase or sentence there is one stress that is stronger than the others. This is the main stress. In this book it is marked with a black box like this:

□　■
A  How are **you**?

■
B  **Fine**.

□　　　　■　　　　□
A  And how are your **wife** and the two

■
**girls**?

There can be more than one main stress in a sentence or phrase. If there is only one syllable in a phrase, then this **must** be the main stress. The main stress is often at the end of the sentence.

**Intonation**

Intonation is the 'music' in the voice. It can go up (**rising** intonation) or down (**falling** intonation). Sometimes it does both (**fall-rise**) or (**rise-fall**). The main intonation always comes with the main stress in the sentence. In this book intonation is shown like this:

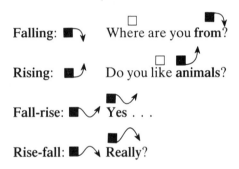

Falling: ■↘　　□　　　　■
　　　　　Where are you **from**?

Rising: ■↗　　Do you like **animals**?

Fall-rise: ■↘↗　Yes . . .

Rise-fall: ■↗↘　Really?

**Word linking**

This often happens when people are speaking fast. The sounds of one word change a little so that we can say it together with the next word more quickly. There are four main types of word linking:

1  When the sound at the end of the first word moves onto the front of the next word:

　　　　　t
Get　　out!

2  When the sound at the end of the first word disappears:

I've **found** the money.

3  When the sound at the end of the first word changes:

　　　　　　/g/
You **should** go home.

4  When there is an extra / w /, / j / or / r / sound between the two words:

Here **we**　　**are**.
　　　　　/ j /

Go　　away!
　　/ w /

**Africa**　　and Asia.
　　　/ r /

# THE PHONEMIC ALPHABET

## Introduction

In this unit you will learn the phonemic symbols used in English. You will practise problem sounds in Units 1–14, not here.

It is important to learn the phonemic alphabet because the relationship between spelling and pronunciation is so irregular in English. So, with the phonemic alphabet, you can work out pronunciation for yourself, using a dictionary. It is also essential for using this book.

The phonemic symbols (and spellings) used in this book are the same as those used in the *Oxford Advanced Learner's Dictionary* (AS Hornby, Oxford University Press.) More or less the same symbols are used in most other modern dictionaries and textbooks.

It is not difficult to learn the phonemic alphabet. However, it is probably best *not* to try to learn all of it together. We advise you to do these five exercises on *separate* days. When you go on to the next exercise, it is a good idea to revise the symbols you have already learned.

## 1  Vowels (1)

1   **T.0.1.A.**  Listen to these pairs of sounds. Can you hear the difference between each pair?

| / i: / | s<u>ee</u> | / ɪ / | b<u>i</u>g |
| / u: / | y<u>ou</u> | / ʊ / | b<u>oo</u>k |
| / ɔ: / | f<u>our</u> | / ɒ / | n<u>o</u>t |

Listen again and try to learn the symbol for each sound.

2   Cover the symbols above and write in the symbol for the words you have just heard.

| / | / | s<u>ee</u> | / | / | b<u>i</u>g |
| / | / | y<u>ou</u> | / | / | b<u>oo</u>k |
| / | / | f<u>our</u> | / | / | n<u>o</u>t |

3   **T.0.1.B.**  Listen and write in the correct symbol for the word that you hear.

|   |   |   |   |
|---|---|---|---|
| /ɒ/<br>a. h<u>o</u>t | / /<br>h. w<u>oo</u>l | / /<br>o. f<u>ee</u>l |
| / /<br>b. h<u>i</u>t | / /<br>i. p<u>u</u>ll | / /<br>p. f<u>i</u>ll |
| / /<br>c. r<u>u</u>de | / /<br>j. p<u>i</u>ll | / /<br>q. b<u>oo</u>t |
| / /<br>d. r<u>ea</u>d | / /<br>k. s<u>i</u>t | / /<br>r. b<u>ou</u>ght |
| / /<br>e. g<u>oo</u>d | / /<br>l. s<u>ea</u>t | / /<br>s. b<u>ea</u>t |
| / /<br>f. G<u>o</u>d | / /<br>m. f<u>a</u>ll | / /<br>t. b<u>i</u>t |
| / /<br>g. w<u>a</u>ll | / /<br>n. f<u>oo</u>l |  |

π—0

## 2 Vowels (2)

1  **T.0.2.A.** Listen to these pairs of sounds. Can you hear the difference between each pair?

/ e / b<u>e</u>d      / æ / c<u>a</u>t
/ ɜː / b<u>ir</u>d     / ə / m<u>o</u>th<u>er</u>
/ ɑː / c<u>ar</u>      / ʌ / <u>u</u>p

Listen again and try to learn the symbol for each sound.

2  Cover the symbols above and write in the correct symbol for the words that you have just heard.

/   / b<u>e</u>d      /   / c<u>a</u>t
/   / b<u>ir</u>d     /   / m<u>o</u>th<u>er</u>
/   / c<u>ar</u>      /   / <u>u</u>p

3  **T.0.2.B.** Listen to the words on the left and circle the correct symbol for the vowel sound on the left.

a. m<u>a</u>n   / ʌ /   / e /  (/ æ /)
b. m<u>e</u>n   / ʌ /   / e /   / æ /
c. f<u>a</u>st  / ʌ /   / æ /   / ɑː /
d. f<u>ir</u>st / ʌ /   / ɜː /  / ɑː /
e. h<u>ea</u>d  / ɜː /  / ə /   / e /
f. h<u>a</u>d   / æ /   / ʌ /   / ɑː /
g. h<u>ear</u>d / ɜː /  / ə /   / ɑː /
h. h<u>ar</u>d  / æ /   / ʌ /   / ɑː /
i. p<u>a</u>ss  / ɑː /  / e /   / æ /
j. p<u>ur</u>se / ɜː /  / ʌ /   / ə /
k. r<u>u</u>n   / ɜː /  / ʌ /   / æ /
l. r<u>a</u>n   / ɜː /  / ʌ /   / æ /

4  **T.0.2.C.** Now listen to these two-syllable words and write in **both** vowel sounds. They may also come from the previous exercise.

/   /   /   /
a. f<u>a</u>th<u>er</u>

/   /   /   /
b. m<u>o</u>th<u>er</u>

/   /   /   /
c. s<u>i</u>st<u>er</u>

/   /   /   /
d. br<u>o</u>th<u>er</u>

/   /   /   /
e. <u>o</u>r<u>a</u>nge

/   /   /   /
f. s<u>u</u>g<u>ar</u>

/   /   /   /
g. b<u>u</u>tt<u>er</u>

/   /   /   /
h. ch<u>o</u>c<u>o</u>late

/   /   /   /
i. s<u>i</u>ng<u>er</u>

/   /   /   /
j. <u>a</u>ctr<u>e</u>ss

/   /   /   /
k. t<u>ea</u>ch<u>er</u>

/   /   /   /
l. d<u>o</u>ct<u>or</u>

## 3 Consonants

1  **T.0.3.A.** Many of the symbols for consonants are easy to recognize. This is how they sound in English:

/ p /   <u>p</u>en     / s /   <u>s</u>it
/ b /   <u>b</u>ig     / z /   <u>z</u>oo
/ t /   <u>t</u>wo     / h /   <u>h</u>ot
/ d /   <u>d</u>oor    / m /   <u>m</u>an
/ k /   <u>c</u>up     / n /   <u>n</u>o
/ g /   <u>g</u>ood    / l /   <u>l</u>ive
/ f /   <u>f</u>at     / r /   <u>r</u>ed
/ v /   lo<u>v</u>e    / w /   <u>w</u>hat

Listen again and mark with a * any of these consonants that sound **very** different in your language. (Most of them will sound a **little** different.) Try to memorize the consonants that you have marked.

2  **T.0.3.B.** These symbols are more difficult:

/ θ /   <u>th</u>in    / ð /   <u>th</u>is
/ ʃ /   <u>sh</u>e     / ʒ /   televi<u>s</u>ion
/ tʃ /  <u>ch</u>air   / dʒ /  <u>j</u>ob
/ ŋ /   si<u>ng</u>    / j /   <u>y</u>es

Listen again and try to learn them.

3  Here are some words in phonemic script. Write in what the word is.

a. / dʒʌmp /  _____

b. / jɔː /  _____

c. / tʃiːp /  _____

d. / θruː /  _____

e. / ˈprɪndʒ /  _____

f. / jʌŋ /  _____

g. / ðæt /  _____

h. / bæŋk /  _____

i. / θɪŋk /  _____

j. / lʌntʃ /  _____

k. / ðiːz /  _____

l. / tʃɜːtʃ /  _____

## 4 Diphthongs (1)

1 | **T.0.4.A.** | Diphthongs are made from two vowel sounds put together. The first of these two sounds is longer and the second is shorter. Some diphthongs are easy to recognize. What do you think these sounds are?

/ eɪ /   da<u>y</u>   / aɪ /   m<u>y</u>
/ ɔɪ /   b<u>oy</u>   / aʊ /   n<u>ow</u>

Listen and check your answers.

Listen again and try to memorize the symbols for these diphthongs.

2 | **T.0.4.B.** | Now listen to the words on the left and say if it is diphthong 1, 2, 3 or 4.

|            | 1 / eɪ / | 2 / aɪ / | 3 / ɔɪ / | 4 / aʊ / |
|------------|----------|----------|----------|----------|
| a.  pay    | √        |          |          |          |
| b.  voice  |          |          | √        |          |
| c.  loud   |          |          |          |          |
| d.  grey   |          |          |          |          |
| e.  die    |          |          |          |          |
| f.  noise  |          |          |          |          |
| g.  house  |          |          |          |          |
| h.  Wales  |          |          |          |          |
| i.  case   |          |          |          |          |
| j.  try    |          |          |          |          |
| k.  coin   |          |          |          |          |
| l.  high   |          |          |          |          |
| m.  flower |          |          |          |          |
| n.  weigh  |          |          |          |          |

π—0

## 5 Diphthongs (2)

1 | **T.0.5.A.** | These diphthongs are more difficult to guess. Try making the two separate vowel sounds and putting them together – what do you think the sounds are?

/ ɪə /   n<u>ea</u>r   / eə /   wh<u>ere</u>
/ əʊ /   g<u>o</u>     / ʊə /   t<u>our</u>*

* This diphthong is very rare – some English speakers never use it. They use / ɔ: / instead.

Listen and see if you guessed correctly.

Listen again and try to memorize the sounds.

2 Cover the symbols above and write them in next to the words you have just heard.

/       /   n<u>ea</u>r     /       /   wh<u>ere</u>

/       /   g<u>o</u>       /       /   t<u>our</u>

3 | **T.0.5.B.** | Listen to the words on the left and match them to the correct transcription on the right, like this:

a. bear      / beɪ /      e. they      / ðeɪ /
   beer      / bɪə /         though    / ðeə /
   bay       / beə /         there     / ðəʊ /

b. toy       / tɔɪ /      f. I'll      / ɔɪl /
   tie       / təʊ /         oil       / aɪl /
   toe       / taɪ /         owl       / aʊl /

c. roll      / reɪl /     g. dear      / daɪ /
   real      / rɪəl /        day       / dɪə /
   rail      / rəʊl /        die       / deɪ /

d. how       / heə /      h. show      / ʃeə /
   hair      / haʊ /         share     / ʃaɪ /
   high      / haɪ /         shy       / ʃəʊ /

π—0

# UNIT 1

## ● Sounds

---

### 1 / s /, / z /, and / ɪz / at the end of words

**All Nationalities**

1 **T.1.1.A.** Listen to the way that the *s* at the end of these verbs is pronounced.

| / s / | / z / | / ɪz / |
|-------|-------|--------|
| starts | lives | finishes |

Can you hear the difference?

2 **T.1.1.B.** Listen to some more verbs and put them into the correct box.

| / s / | / z / | / ɪz / |
|-------|-------|--------|
| likes | owns | |
| | | |
| | | |
| | | |

Listen again and repeat. Pay attention to the pronunciation of the final *s*.

3 Complete the rules:

a. If a verb ends with the sounds / s /, / z /, / ʃ /, / tʃ / or / dʒ / the final *s* is pronounced . . . . . .

b. If a verb ends with any other voiceless consonant ( / p /, / t /, / k /, / f / or / θ / ) the final *s* is pronounced . . . . . .

c. If a verb ends with any other voiced consonant ( / b /, / d /, / g /, / v /, / ð /, / l /, / m /, / n / or / ŋ / ), or a vowel sound, the final *s* is pronounced . . . . . .

4 The above rules are the same for *s* at the end of nouns too. Decide how the final *s* is pronounced in the nouns below and then mark it / s /, / z / or / ɪz /.

| /z/ | /ɪz/ |
|-----|------|
| suburbs | chances |
| houses | bedrooms |
| gardens | hours |
| weeks | buses |
| pets | sports |
| children's | miles |

**T.1.1.C.** Listen and check your answers.

Practise saying the words. Make sure that you pronounce the final *s* correctly.

## 2 Groups of consonants with 's'
Ⓔ Ⓖⓡ Ⓘ Ⓣⓡ

1 | **T.1.2.A.** | Listen to the words below. They all have *s* and another consonant at the beginning. Is the *s* pronounced / s / or / z /?

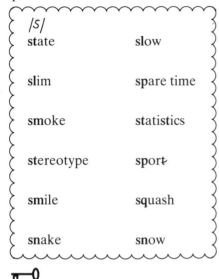

/s/

| state | slow |
| slim | spare time |
| smoke | statistics |
| stereotype | sport |
| smile | squash |
| snake | snow |

2 Work with a partner. Put the sentences below into the correct order. There may be more than one possible answer – how many possibilities can you find?

   a. but/speak/speak/Spanish/Swedish/I/don't/unfortunately/I

   b. Steve/doesn't/slowly/very/speaks/he/?

   c. and/snowing/Scandinavia/it/Switzerland/was/Sunday/Spain/on/in

   d. sports/started/he/playing/smoking/has/stopped/and

   e. spare/Stephanie/squash/plays/and/time/in/swimming/her/goes

3 | **T.1.2.B.** | Listen and compare your answers to those on the tape.
Practise saying the sentences as fast as possible. Make sure that you pronounce the words beginning with *s* correctly.

## ● Connected speech

## 3 Contraction of *be* with the Present Continuous

1 | **T.1.3.A.** | Listen to *be* in the contracted form.

| | |
|---|---|
| I'*m* | It'*s* |
| You'*re* | We'*re* |
| He'*s* | They'*re* |
| She'*s* | |

Listen again and repeat.

2 | **T.1.3.B.** | With the Present Continuous, it is sometimes very difficult to hear *be*, especially when people are speaking quickly, and sometimes students miss it out. Listen to these two foreign students – one of them says *be* and one of them does not:

  \*I living in England at the moment.
  I'*m* living in England at the moment.

  In my class we'*re* studying for an exam.
  \*In my class we studying for an exam.

  Can you hear the difference?

3 | **T.1.3.C.** | Listen to this student – he says ten sentences. For each sentence mark the box below with a tick ✓ if he remembers *be* and a X if he forgets it.

a. ☐   b. ☐   c. ☐   d. ☐   e. ☐

f. ☐   g. ☐   h. ☐   i. ☐   j. ☐

| **T.1.3.D.** | Listen to the correct sentences and repeat them. Pronounce *be* correctly.

## 4 The weak form of *do*

Auxiliary verbs like *do* often have a **weak** and a **strong** form.

    **Weak** form: *Do you . . .* / dʒʊ / or / dʒə /
    **Strong** form: *Do* / du: /

1 | **T.1.4.A.** | Listen to the dialogue on the next page and underline the weak form of *do* like this ∿∿∿ and the strong form like this _____.

Do you like sport?

Yes, I do. I love it!

Which sports do you play?

Oh, I don't play any myself, but I watch them all on TV!

When is the **strong** form used?
When is the **weak** form used?

2  | T.1.4.B. |  Practise saying the weak form / dʒʊ / or / dʒə /. Start at the end of the question like this:

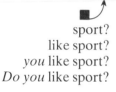

sport?
like sport?
*you* like sport?
*Do you* like sport?

3  | T.1.4.C. |  Look at the pictures below and make the questions. Remember that with some sports *play* is used and with some *go* is used. Listen and check your questions on the tape. Pronounce the weak form of *Do you . . .?* correctly.

| a. | b. | c. |
| d. | e. | f. |
| g. | h. | i. |

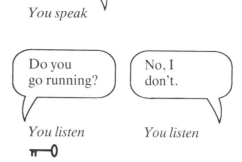

Do you go running?

*You speak*

Do you go running?

No, I don't.

*You listen*          *You listen*

4  Try to guess what sports the other students in your class play. Ask them and find out if you guessed correctly.

## ● Intonation and sentence stress

Do this exercise after the Reading on pages 4 and 5 of the Student's Book.

## 5  Showing surprise

1  | T.1.5.A. |  In the following dialogues A has just read the article about the McCartneys on page 4 of the Student's Book. He is telling B some of the interesting facts that he discovered.

Listen and write in what B says.

a.   **A** Paul McCartney lives in a two-bedroom house!

    **B** _____

b.   **A** Linda McCartney has a 17-year old daughter!

    **B** _____

c.   **A** The McCartneys are all vegetarians!

    **B** _____

d.   **A** Paul McCartney knows how to bake bread!

    **B** _____

e.   **A** Linda drives a very small car!

    **B** _____

f.  A  Linda does all the cooking herself!

    B  _____

g.  A  Paul and Linda both love football!
    B  _____

h.  A  Linda much prefers living in the country!

    B  _____

i.  A  In the evening the McCartneys usually
       just watch TV!

    B  _____

🔑—0

2  T.1.5.B.  Speaker **B** is surprised by what **A** says, so his intonation goes up:

■⤴
Does he?

Practise the intonation. Try exaggerating first like this:

■⤴        ■⤴        ■⤴
Does he?  Does he?  Does he?

■⤴        ■⤴        ■⤴
Does she? Does she? Does she?

■⤴        ■⤴        ■⤴
Are they? Are they? Are they?

3  ◀  T.1.5.A.  Listen again and repeat **B**'s part.

_____

Do this exercise before the Speaking Activity on page 5 of the Student's Book.

## 6  Main stress and intonation in *Wh*-questions

T.1.6.A.  Sentences have words which are **stressed** and words which are **unstressed**:

☐        ☐        ☐        ☐
Excuse me, where can I buy a newspaper?

Some of the stresses are stronger than others – they are the main stresses (marked ■):

■        ☐        ☐        ■
Excuse me, where can I buy a newspaper?

1  T.1.6.B.  Here are some more questions that you might ask if you arrive in a new town. Listen and mark the main stresses like this ■.

a.  Excuse me, where can I get stamps?

b.  Excuse me, where's the nearest post office?

c.  Excuse me, where's the nearest bank?

d.  What time does it open?

e.  What time does it close?

f.  Where can I find cheap accommodation?

g.  How much does a single room cost?

h.  What's the address?

i.  What's the telephone number?

Where is the main stress in all of the questions?

Does the intonation go **up** or **down**? Is this the same or different in your language?

🔑—0

To say the questions with the correct intonation, you should **start high** and go **down** on the **main stress**. This is to make you sound more polite and interested.

2  T.1.6.C.  To practise start by exaggerating, like this:

■⤵⤴  ☐  ☐  ■⤵
Excuse me, where can I buy a newspaper?

■⤵⤴  ☐  ☐  ■⤵
Excuse me, where can I buy a newspaper?

■⤵⤴  ☐  ☐  ■⤵
Excuse me, where can I buy a newspaper?

Listen to the questions again and repeat them. Remember that if your intonation doesn't start *high*, you will probably sound bored and impolite.

# ● Word focus

## 7 Word stress and the sound / ə /

Look at the dictionary entry for the word *average*. As well as the meaning, you can find the pronunciation of the word, including the stress:

> **av·er·age** /ˈævərɪdʒ/ *n* **1** [C] result of adding several amounts together and dividing the total by the number of amounts: *The average of 4, 5 and 9 is 6.* **2** [U] standard or level regarded as usual: *These marks are well above/below average.*

● average

1 Below are the dictionary entries for some more words from this unit. First check the meaning, if necessary, and then mark the stress in the same way.

> **busi·ness** /ˈbɪznɪs/ *n* **1** [C, U] one's usual occupation; profession: *He tries not to let (his) business interfere with his home life.* **2** [U] **(a)** buying and selling (esp as a profession);

business

> **com·pany** /ˈkʌmpənɪ/ *n* **1** [U] being together with another or others: *I enjoy his company,* ie I like being with him. ○ *be good, bad, etc company,* ie be pleasant, unpleasant, etc to be with. **2** [U] group of people together; number of guests: *She told the assembled company what had happened.* ○ *We're expecting company* (ie guests, visitors) *next week.*

company

> **en·gin·eer** /ˌendʒɪˈnɪə(r)/ *n* **1** person who designs, builds or maintains engines, machines, bridges, railways, mines, etc: *a civil/mining/electrical/mechanical engineer.*

engineer

> **en·ter·tain·ment** *n* **1** [U] entertaining or being entertained: *the entertainment of a group of foreign visitors* ○ *He fell in the water, much to the entertainment of the children.*

entertainment

> **in·forma·tion** /ˌɪnfəˈmeɪʃn/ *n* [U] **1** informing or being informed: *For your information* (ie This is sth you may wish to know), *the library is on the first floor.* ○ (ironic) *I'm perfectly able to look after myself, for your information.* ○ (fml) *My information is that* (ie I have been told that) *they have all left.* **2** ~ **(on/about sb/sth)** facts told.

information

> **journal** /ˈdʒɜːnl/ *n* **1** newspaper or periodical, esp **journ·al·ist** /-nəlɪst/ *n* person whose profession is journalism: *He's a journalist on the 'Daily Telegraph'.* Cf REPORTER (REPORT¹).

journalist

> **oc·cu·pa·tion** /ˌɒkjʊˈpeɪʃn/ *n* **1** [U] **(a)** action of occupying; state of being occupied (OCCUPY 1): *the occupation of a house by a family.* **(b)** taking and keeping possession: *a country under enemy occupation* ○ *an army of occupation.*

occupation

> **pop·ular** /ˈpɒpjʊlə(r)/ *adj* **1 (a)** liked, admired or enjoyed by many people: *a popular politician* ○ *Jeans are popular among the young.* ○ *Jogging is a popular form of exercise.* **(b)** ~ **with sb** liked, admired or enjoyed by sb: *measures popular with the electorate* ○ (infml) *I'm not very popular with the boss* (ie He is annoyed with me) *at the moment.*

popular

> **pro·mo·tion** /prəˈməʊʃn/ *n* **1 (a)** [U] raising or being raised to a higher rank or position: *gain/win promotion* ○ *If you are successful, you can expect promotion.* ○ [attrib] *promotion prospects.* **(b)** [C] instance of this: *The new job is a promotion for her.*

promotion

> **ve·get·arian** /ˌvedʒɪˈteərɪən/ *n* person who, for humane, religious or health reasons, eats no meat: [attrib] *a vegetarian meal, diet, restaurant.* Cf VEGAN.

vegetarian

2 In many of the words you will notice the sound / ə /, or schwa. This is the most common vowel sound in English. Look at the words again and mark the schwa sounds:

/ ə /
average

What do you notice about the word stress and the schwas?

3 T.1.7.A. Practise saying the words, making sure that the stress and schwa sounds are correct.

If you have problems with the stress, try starting with the stressed syllable, like this:

| ● | ● | ● |
|---|---|---|
| neer | tainment | mation |
| gineer | tertainment | formation |
| engineer | entertainment | information |

To make the sound / ə /, try relaxing your mouth. The sound is made in the middle of the mouth. Your lips should look like this:

/ ə /

T.1.7.B. Listen and check your pronunciation of the words of the dictionary entries in 1.

## ● Everyday English

## 8 Saying addresses and telephone numbers

1 **T.1.8.A.** A bank clerk is asking customers their addresses and telephone numbers. Listen and complete the forms below.

a.
Name _Karen Norman_____

Address _____

_____

Tel. no. _____

b.
Name _Philip Wood_____

Address _____

_____

Tel. no. _____

c.
Name _Sally Ann Bailey_____

Address _____

_____

Tel. no. _____

d.
Name _Paul Crocker_____

Address _____

_____

Tel. no. _____

2 **T.1.8.B.** Listen to the bank clerk's questions. This time you take the part of the customers.

3 Now find out the addresses and telephone numbers of some of the other students in your class.

# UNIT 2

## ● Sounds

Do this exercise after reading the Fact File on page 7 of the Student's Book.

**1** The sounds / v / and / w /
(D) (H) (J) (Tr)

To make the sound / v / your **top teeth** should touch the inside of your **bottom lip** like this:

/ v /

To make the sound / w / your teeth **don't** touch your lips. Your lips should be hard and round like this:

/ w /

If you have problems with the sound / w / you can try starting with / u: / like this:

uuu → where
uu → where
u → where

In English, if a word is spelt with the letter *v* it is pronounced with the sound / v /. If it is spelt with the letter *w* it is almost always pronounced / w /.

1  Look at the Fact File about Willi Hoffman on page 7 of the Student's Book and find all the words that contain the sound / v / and all the words that contain the sound / w /. Write them in the columns. (Notice that in German *Willi* is pronounced with a / v /.)

| / v / | / w / |
| --- | --- |
|  |  |
|  |  |
|  |  |
|  |  |
|  |  |

**T.2.1.A.**  Listen and check your answers.

π—O
Listen again and practise saying the words correctly.

2  **T.2.1.B.**  Here are some phrases from the Fact File. Practise reading them aloud, paying attention to your pronunciation of *v* and *w*.

. . . higher producti**v**ity **w**ill
    increase exports . . .
. . . he belie**v**es in nuclear
    po**w**er . . .
. . . he thinks nuclear **w**eapons
    are necessary . . .
. . . to keep **w**orld peace . . .
. . . he **w**orks at least twel**v**e
    hours a day . . .
. . . he likes **w**atching
    tele**v**ision . . .

Listen and check your pronunciation.

3  Spelling and silent *w*
There is one word in the Fact File on page 7 which is spelt with a *w* that is **not pronounced** (not Willi!) – can you find it?

Here are some more words beginning with *wr* and *wh*. Decide which of these words have a silent *w*. Use a dictionary if you are not sure.

> wrong whether wrist
> whole who wrinkled
> whip where wreck

What is the rule for words beginning with *wr-*?
What is the rule for words beginning with *wh-*?

🗝

# ● Connected speech

## 2 Weak forms of *Would you . . .?* and *Do you . . .?*

When we speak quickly *Would you . . .?* and *Do you . . .?* are often pronounced with weak forms:

**Would you . . .?** / wʊdʒʊ / or / wʊdʒə /

**Do you . . .?** / dʒʊ / or / dʒə /

1 **T.2.2.A.** Listen to the dialogue between Bob and Anna in a disco and fill in the missing words.

**Bob** _____ you like to dance?

**Anna** No, thanks.

**Bob** _____ you like cocktails?

**Anna** Yes, I do.

**Bob** _____ you like something to drink?

**Anna** No, thanks.

**Bob** _____ you like hamburgers?

**Anna** Yes, I do.

**Bob** _____ you like something to eat?

**Anna** No, thanks.

**Bob** _____ you like a cigarette?

**Anna** No, thanks.

**Bob** _____ you like this music?

**Anna** Yes, I do.

**Bob** _____ you like the disc jockey?

**Anna** He's _____.

Are the weak forms used in the questions?

What about in Anna's answers?

🗝

2 **T.2.2.B.** To practise these weak forms, start at the end of the question like this:

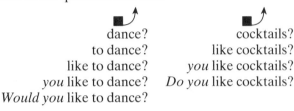

| | |
|---|---|
| dance? | cocktails? |
| to dance? | like cocktails? |
| like to dance? | *you* like cocktails? |
| *you* like to dance? | *Do you* like cocktails? |
| *Would you* like to dance? | |

Listen again and repeat Bob's questions. Pay attention to your pronunciation of the weak forms.

3 Practise reading the dialogue with a partner. Try to add some more questions with *Would you like . . .?* and *Do you like . . .?*

Do this exercise after the Reading on pages 10 and 11 of the Student's Book.

## 3 Weak form of *at*

1 **T.2.3.A.** Look at the television programmes on page 10 of your Student's Book. **A** and **B** are talking about them. Listen and fill in what they say.

🗝

How is the word *at* pronounced?

🗝

Notice that because **B** is speaking quickly, many of the words link together:

It's on at nine o'clock.

2 **T.2.3.B.** Practise the weak forms and linking. You can start at the end of the sentence, like this:

☐ ◼↘
nine twenty-five.
/ ət /
*at* nine twenty-five.
*on at* nine twenty-five.
It's *on at* nine twenty-five.

3 **T.2.3.C.** Listen to the questions about the following programmes and respond giving times in the same way as **B**. You will need to look at page 10 of the Student's Book.

| Question | Answer |
|---|---|
| a. *Cagney and Lacey's on BBC 1, isn't it?* | *Yes, that's right, it's on at 9.25.* |
| *You listen* | *You speak* |

Yes, that's right, it's on at 9.25.

*You listen*

a. *Cagney and Lacey*
b. *Gardener's World*
c. *Postman Pat*
d. *Countdown*
e. *The Big Shot*
f. *Family Fortunes*
g. *Dangermouse*
h. *Newsnight*

π—0

---

## 4 Contractions and weak forms

1 **T.2.4.** Listen to the sentences and write how many words you hear in the box on the right. **Contractions** (e.g. *don't*) are two words which sound like one word when spoken together quickly.

a. How _____ [6]

_____

go skiing?

b. _____ ☐

borrow _____ magazine?

---

c. _____ anything ☐

good _____ ?

d. What time _____ ☐

_____ ?

e. I _____ meals. ☐

f. I _____ ☐

a meal.

g. _____ good ☐

_____ athletics?

h. I _____ ☐

running.

2 Listen again and write the missing words into the blanks.

π—0

3 Listen again and practise saying the sentences. Remember the pronunciation of *Do you . . .?* / dʒʊ / or / dʒə /, *Would you . . .?* / wʊdʒə / and *at* / ət /.

How are *to*, *for*, and *Are you . . .?* pronounced?

π—0

## ● Intonation

---

## 5 Sounding enthusiastic

1 **T.2.5.A.** Listen to the dialogue between **A** (an English person) and **B** (a visitor from abroad). Fill in the blanks in **A**'s questions.

A Do you like ............................................? 
B Yeah, it's great!

A Would you like ......................................? 
B Yes, please!

A Do you like ............................................? 
B Yeah, they're great!

A Would you like ......................................? 
B Yes, please!

A Do you like ...........................................?
B Yeah, they're great!

A Would you like ......................................?
B Yes, please!

A Do you like ...........................................?
B Yeah, it's great!

A Would you like ......................................?
B Er . . . no, thanks!

What do you notice about the visitor's intonation?
Why do you think she is speaking like this?

2 **T.2.5.B.** Practise the intonation. You can first exaggerate like this:

Yeah, it's great!  Yeah, it's great!  Yeah, it's great!

Yes, please!  Yes, please!  Yes, please!

*Remember that if your intonation is flat, you will probably sound **bored** or **impolite**.*

3 **T.2.5.C.** Listen to the questions again and this time you respond. Pay attention to your intonation.

---

## 6 Rising and falling intonation in single words

*When we **answer** questions with yes or no, our intonation normally goes **down**. But sometimes we use these words to **ask questions** – then our intonation goes up.*

1 **T.2.6.** Listen to these dialogues and mark the words ■↘ if the intonation goes **down** (because the speaker is just answering a question) or ■↗ if the intonation goes **up** (because the speaker is **asking** a question).

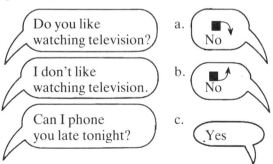

Do you like watching television?  a. No
I don't like watching television.  b. No
Can I phone you late tonight?  c. Yes

---

You can phone me as late as you like.  d. Yes
e. John  f. Yes
g. John  h. Yes
i. Okay  j. Yes, fine thanks.
k. Okay
How's your wife?

2 Listen again and practise saying the words with the correct intonation.

---

## 7 Rising and falling intonation in questions

1 **T.2.7.** Listen to the questions and decide if the intonation goes **up** or **down** at the end. Mark them ■↗ or ■↘.

a. Do you like American films? ■↗

b. Where would you like to go this evening? ■↘

c. Would you like to see a play? ■

d. Would you like to watch the news? ■

e. What sort of books do you read? ■

f. Do you like cooking? ■

g. Do you play tennis? ■

h. Would you like something to drink? ■

i. What would you like for dinner? ■

j. Which newspaper do you read? ■

2 What type of questions go **up**?

What type of questions go **down**?

3 Listen again and practise the questions. Pay attention to your intonation.

## ● Word focus

---

## 8 Stress in words ending in *-sion* and *-tion*

1 In English there are lots of words that end in *-sion* and *-tion*. Look up the words below in a dictionary, marking the **stress** and **schwa sounds** like this:

/ə/   /ə/ ● /ə/
accommodation

> ambition         occupation
> nation           description
> conversation     revision

What do you notice about the **position** of the stressed syllable?

What do you notice about the pronunciation of *-sion* and *-tion*?

2 │ **T.2.8.A.** │ Practise the words starting with the stressed syllable, like this:

> ● dation │ ● bition │ ● sation
> modation │ ambition │ versation
> commodation │ │ conversation
> accommodation

3 Work out the pronunciation of the following words:

> competition      vision
> reception        television
> decision         station

│ **T.2.8.B.** │ Listen and check your answers.

---

## 9 Entertainment vocabulary

1 The words in phonemic script below are all related to entertainment. Can you transcribe them?

a. / kɑːˈtuːn /   *cartoon*

b. / ˈkɒmədɪ /  _____

c. / kəˈmiːdɪən /  _____

d. / dɒkjʊˈmentrɪ /  _____

e. / ˈprəʊgræm /  _____

f. / kwɪz /  _____

g. / ˈθɪətə /  _____

h. / ˈwestən /  _____

2 │ **T.2.9.** │ Look at the transcription again and then mark the stressed syllable like this ●. Use the phonemic transcription to work out how the words are pronounced and then listen and check your answers.

## ● Everyday English

---

## 10 Saying the time

There are two different ways of saying the time in English:

10.45     *or*   quarter to eleven
7.00 a.m.  *or*   seven o'clock in the morning
7.00 p.m.  *or*   seven o'clock in the evening

1 │ **T.2.10.** │ Listen and answer the questions on the tape like this:

**Question**                          **Answer**

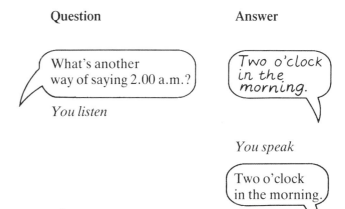

2 Work with a partner. Ask and answer the same type of questions.

11

# UNIT 3

## ● Sounds

### 1 The sounds / θ / and / ð /

(D) (F) (H) (I) (J) (P) (Tr)

To make the sounds / θ / and / ð / your **tongue** should touch the **back of your teeth**. If you find this difficult try putting your finger in front of your mouth and touching it with your tongue like this:

For the sound / ð / you should use your voice – for the sound / θ / you should not.

1   **T.3.1.**   Listen and practise these words:

| / θ / | / ð / |
|---|---|
| thick | this |
| thin | those |
| thinks | these |
| thirty | there |
| three | then |
| theatre | with |
| both | mother |
| path | father |
| teeth | together |
| healthy | although |

2   For more practice, now do point 1 of exercise 9 on page 17 of this book.

## 2 Pronunciation of -ed past tenses

**All Nationalities**

There are three different pronunciations of -ed in regular past tense verbs:

| / d / | / t / | / ɪd / |
|---|---|---|
| phoned | cooked | landed |

1   **T.3.2.A.**   Listen to these past tense verbs and put them in the right column, according to the pronunciation of -ed. You will hear each verb twice.

| | |
|---|---|
| helped | discovered |
| offered | looked |
| reached | called |
| saved | tried |
| missed | invited |
| started | asked |
| lived | jumped |
| needed | waited |

| / t / | / d / |
|---|---|
| | |
| | |
| | |
| | |

| / ɪd / |
|---|
| |
| |
| |

⊓━0

**2** Listen again, and repeat the verbs with the correct pronunciation.

Complete the rules:

a. If a verb itself ends in *t* or *d* the final -*ed* is pronounced

..........

b. If a verb ends in a **voiceless** consonant (/ p /, / s /, / k /, / f /, / ʃ /, / tʃ / or / θ /) the final -*ed* is pronounced .......... .

c. If a verb ends in a **voiced** consonant ( b /, / g /, / l /, / z /, / v /, / dʒ /, / ð /, / m /, / n /, or / ŋ /) or a vowel sound, the final -*ed* is pronounced ....... .

🔑

**3** ⬚T.3.2.B.⬚ Listen to these sentences and write / t /, / d / or / ɪd / in the box to show the pronunciation of -*ed*.

a. ⬚Id⬚ Last year we decided not to go abroad.

⬚ ⬚ We rented a lovely cottage in Wales.

⬚ ⬚ It rained every day.

b. ⬚ ⬚ We hitchhiked across Europe.

⬚ ⬚ We stayed with friends in Paris.

⬚ ⬚ We camped outside Rome.

c. ⬚ ⬚ I worked all last summer.

⬚ ⬚ I wanted a new car.

⬚ ⬚ I saved up a lot of money.

d. ⬚ ⬚ Last summer I visited my cousin in New York.

⬚ ⬚ I really enjoyed it.

⬚ ⬚ I travelled all over America too.

🔑

Listen again and practise saying the sentences. Pay attention to your pronunciation of the past tense verbs.

# ● Connected speech

**3** Weak forms of *was* and *were* with the Past Continuous

**1** Last month Mr and Mrs Bailey went away for a holiday. They left their teenage children at home. Because of bad weather they came home early. This is the scene they found when they arrived home.

⬚T.3.3.⬚ Listen and fill in the gaps.

a. Their teenage children _____

_____

b. Their daughter Sue _____

_____

c. Their son Philip _____

_____

d. Their son Peter _____

_____

13

e. Philip's girlfriend _____

_____

f. Sue's boyfriend _____

g. Peter's girlfriend _____

_____

h. Two of Philip's friends _____

_____

i. Two of Sue's friends _____

_____

2  Look at the picture. Can you say who all the people
   are?

3  Listen again. How are *was* and *were* pronounced?
   ⊓—0

   Practise saying the sentences. Pay attention to your
   pronunciation of *was* and *were*.

4  Work with a partner. Try to memorize what is in
   the picture and then close your book. Ask each
   other questions, like this:

   > What was Sue doing?

   > She was dancing on the table.

● **Intonation and sentence stress**

**4** Showing interest

> I was working in France last summer.

> Were you?

> I earned lots of money.

> Did you?

A                          B

1  **T.3.4.A.**  Look at these short dialogues between **A**
   and **B**. Listen and write short questions in the
   spaces.

a. ☐  A Last summer we hitchhiked all the way
          to Turkey.

      B _Did you_____ ?

b. ☐  A Yes, and it only took three days.

      B _____ ?

c. ☐  A We were in Hawaii this time last week.

      B _____ ?

d. ☐  A Mmm. It was absolutely fantastic.

      B _____ ?

e. ☐  A John and Vera had a lovely holiday in
          Corfu.

      B _____ ?

f. ☐  A Yes, and John took some lovely
          photographs.

      B _____ ?

g. ☐  A We spent our holidays in Britain this year.

      B _____ ?

h. ☐  A Yes, but it was more expensive than
          going abroad.

      B _____ ?

i. ☐  A June and her husband went to Scotland
          to play golf last week.

      B _____ ?

j. ☐  A Yes. June had a wonderful time.

      B _____ ?

   ⊓—0

2  Listen again. In some of the dialogues **B** sounds **interested** in what **A** is saying and in some she does not. If **B** sounds interested write *I* in the box on the left and if she sounds uninterested write *U* in the box on the left.

3  | T.3.4.B. |  To show that you are interested and want to hear more, your intonation should start high, go down, and then go up at the end.

Remember, if your intonation is flat you can sound bored.

You can practise by first exaggerating, like this:

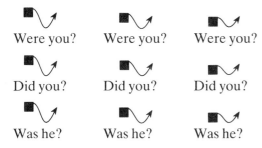

4  | T.3.4.C. |  Listen to some people talking about their holidays. Ask short questions. Try to show that you are interested and want to hear more.

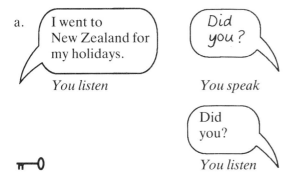

Do this exercise after the Picture Story on pages 14 and 15 of the Student's Book.

## 5  Stressed and unstressed words

1  | T.3.5. |  Listen to these sentences from the story on pages 14 and 15 of the Student's Book. Mark the stressed syllables with a box □.

☐ ☐ ☐ ☐
On the fourteenth of January nineteen seventy-
☐ ☐ ☐ ☐
eight, Mrs Brewin was working in her garden.

Her cat, Henry, was playing around her.

It climbed a tree in the garden and couldn't get

down, so she called the Fire Brigade.

While she was waiting for them to arrive, she

offered him some fish to try to get him down.

2  What kind of words, generally, are **stressed**? What kind of words are **not stressed**?

3  Listen again and read along with the tape. You do not need to pronounce all the words clearly – you can just *mumble* like this:

mm mm MM-mm mm MM-mm-mm MM-mm-MM-mm-MM, mm-mm MM-mm mm MM-mm mm mm MM-mm

But pay attention to stress and rhythm.

Practise reading the passage *to yourself*, still paying attention to stress and rhythm.

4  Look at the rest of the story on pages 14 and 15. Work out the stress and rhythm in the same way. Then practise reading it aloud.

## ● Word focus

### 6 Word stress in adjectives ending in -ous

Notice the stress in these adjectives:

● •     • ● •     • ● • •
fa-mous   am-bi-tious   con-tin-u-ous

1 Put the words in the box into the right columns, according to the number of syllables, and the stress pattern. If there are some words you don't know, try to guess where the stress is, without using a dictionary.

| | |
|---|---|
| curious | hilarious |
| dangerous | jealous |
| delicious | poisonous |
| disastrous | precious |
| famous | religious |
| generous | ridiculous |

| 1 ● • | 2 ● • • |
|---|---|
| | |

| 3 • ● • | 4 • ● • • |
|---|---|
| | |

Are your guesses correct? Use a dictionary to check your answers. You can also check the meaning of new words at the same time.

🔑

2 **T.3.6.** Listen, and practise saying the words with the tape.

Do this exercise after the Reading and Language Work on page 16 of the Student's Book.

### 7 Money vocabulary

1 All the words below come from the cut up newspaper article about Linda Smaje. Transcribe them and mark the stress like this ●.

/ ˈmʌnɪ /   _money_

/ ˈkredɪtkɑːd / _____

/ ˈfaɪnænsˈkʌmpnɪ / _____

/ ɜː nz/ _____

/ ˈbɒrəʊd / _____

/ ləʊn / _____

/ ˈbæŋkrəpsɪ / _____

/ ˈmʌnθlɪˈsteɪtmənt / _____

🔑

2 **T.3.7.** Use the phonemic transcription to work out the correct pronunciation. Then listen and check.

3 Work in pairs. Write a story of less than 40 words including as many of the words above as you can. Read your story to the rest of the class, paying attention to your pronunciation of these words. Which pair managed to use the most words?

## ● Everyday English

### 8 Saying prices

1 **T.3.8.A.** Listen to these prices and practise saying them.

2 | T.3.8.B. | Look at the pictures and answer the questions on the tape like this:

| Question | Answer |
|---|---|
| Excuse me for asking, but how much did your handbag cost? | *It was £19.99 actually.* |
| *You listen* | *You speak* |
| | It was £19.99 actually. |
| | *You listen* |

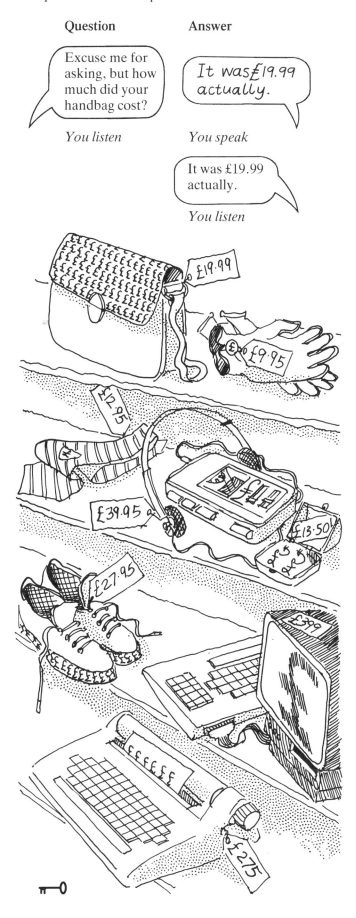

## 9 Saying dates

1 | T.3.9.A. | Listen and practise saying these dates. Make sure that you pronounce / θ / and / ð / correctly.

10 May 1983

3 March 1934

13 December 1793

12 February 1903

24 July 1963

30 September 1833

2 Try to guess when these famous people were born, by matching up the people and the dates like this:

| | | |
|---|---|---|
| a. | Marie Antoinette | 6 March 1475 |
| b. | Napoleon Bonaparte | 23 April 1564 |
| c. | Michelangelo Buonarotti | 2 November 1755 |
| d. | Agatha Christie | 15 August 1769 |
| e. | Greta Garbo | 5 May 1818 |
| f. | Mikhail Gorbachev | 25 October 1881 |
| g. | Karl Marx | 15 September 1890 |
| h. | Marilyn Monroe | 18 September 1905 |
| i. | Pablo Picasso | 13 October 1925 |
| j. | Elvis Presley | 1 June 1926 |
| k. | William Shakespeare | 2 March 1931 |
| l. | Margaret Thatcher | 8 January 1938 |

3 | T.3.9.B. | Listen and check your answers.

Listen again and repeat, paying attention to your pronunciation of the dates.

4 Find out when the other people in your class were born.

# UNIT 4

## ● Sounds

### 1 Distinguishing the sounds / k /, / g /, and / w /
Ⓔ Ⓖⓡ

1 ⟦ **T.4.1.A.** ⟧ Listen to the sounds at the beginning of these three words:

a. could    b. good    c. would

**Can you hear the difference?**

2 ⟦ **T.4.1.B.** ⟧ Listen and tick (√) the sound that you hear.

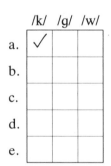

|     | /k/ | /g/ | /w/ |
|-----|-----|-----|-----|
| a.  | √   |     |     |
| b.  |     |     |     |
| c.  |     |     |     |
| d.  |     |     |     |
| e.  |     |     |     |

|     | /k/ | /g/ | /w/ |
|-----|-----|-----|-----|
| f.  |     |     |     |
| g.  |     |     |     |
| h.  |     |     |     |
| i.  |     |     |     |
| j.  |     |     |     |

To make the sound / w / your lips should be hard and round, like this:

/ w /

If you have problems with this sound try starting with the sound / u: / first:

uuu → would   uu → would   u → would

To begin the sounds / k / and / g /, the back of your tongue should touch the top of your mouth at the back.

/ k /

/ g /

/ k / is **voiceless** and / g / is **voiced**.

At the beginning of words, / k / has a lot of **aspiration** in English. You can practise this by holding a piece of paper in front of your mouth when you make the sound. The air that comes out of your mouth should make the piece of paper move.

3 Listen again and practise saying the words.

### 2 *Could* or *Would*?
Ⓔ Ⓖⓡ

1 ⟦ **T.4.2.** ⟧ Listen and complete the requests with either *Could* or *Would*.

a. _____ you tell me the time?

b. _____ you lend me your pencil?

c. _____ you do me a favour?

d. _____ you take this upstairs with you?

e. _____ you fetch my glasses from the kitchen?

f. _____ I borrow some money?

g. _____ you help me to carry this?

h. _____ you read this through?

π—0

2  Practise saying the sentences paying attention to the sounds / k / and / w / at the beginning of the words *Could* and *Would*. Remember that your intonation should sound polite.

# ● Connected speech

## 3 Contractions and weak forms

1  **T.4.3.** Listen to the sentences and count the words. Write the number in the box on the left. (*I'll* = two words)

a.  [8]
_____ window _____ ?

b.  [ ]
_____ shops _____ .

c.  [ ]
_____ television _____ ?

d.  [ ]
_____ airport _____ .

e.  [ ]
_____ coffee _____ .

f.  [ ]
_____ red wine _____ ?

π—0

2  Listen again and write in the missing words.

π—0

3  Practise saying the sentences.

# ● Intonation

## 4 Showing politeness in requests and responses

When we ask people to do things the words that we choose are very important:

*Could* you *turn* the radio down?

is more polite than

*Turn* the radio down!

But the **intonation** is also very important.

1  **T.4.4.A.** Listen to the first two sentences below. The words are the same but **A** sounds **polite** and **B** sounds **rude**. Can you hear the difference?

2  Listen to the other sentences and mark them  P  if they sound **polite** and  R  if they sound **rude**.

1. **A** Could you close the door?  P

   **B** Could you close the door?  R

2. **A** Would you mind waiting for a moment?

   **B** Would you mind waiting for a moment?

3. **A** Do you think you could help me?

   **B** Do you think you could help me?

4. **A** Can you phone back later?

   **B** Can you phone back later?

5. **A** Would you mind carrying this bag?

   **B** Would you mind carrying this bag?

6. **A** Could you do the washing up?

   **B** Could you do the washing up?

π—0

3 T.4.4.B. Listen again and repeat the **polite** sentences.

When you agree to a request, your intonation should also sound polite and interested. To do this your voice should start high.

To practise, first try exaggerating like this:

Yes, of course!  Yes, of course!

Yes, of course!

4  T.4.4.C.  Listen and reply **only** when the intonation of the request is polite.

a. **Polite question**      **Answer**

Could you give me a light?

*You listen*

Yes, of course!

*You speak*

Yes, of course!

*You listen*

b. **Rude question**

Would you mind opening the window?

**Answer**

There is *no* answer here.

c. Could you give me a lift to work?

d. Do you think you could pass me the salt?

e. Could you show me the station on the map?

f. Do you think you could give me some change?

g. Could you tell me where the Ladies' toilet is?

h. Could you wait for me?

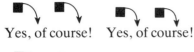

---

## 5 Making polite requests

1  T.4.5.  Look at the pictures and listen to the prompt words. Make polite requests like this, paying attention to your intonation:

**A beer**

Do you think you could bring me a beer please?

*You speak*

Do you think you could bring me a beer please?

*You listen*

Certainly!

*You listen*

B MENU
C
D
E
F
G
H BILL

Before doing this exercise do point 1 of exercise 9 on page 22.

## 6 Showing degrees of enthusiasm

1  T.4.6.A.  Listen to the two dialogues below. Speaker B says *yes* in a different way in each case. Can you hear the difference? What does this show about her feelings?

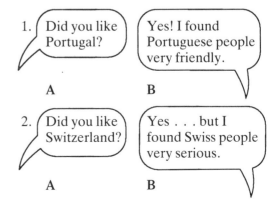

1. Did you like Portugal?

A

Yes! I found Portuguese people very friendly.

B

2. Did you like Switzerland?

A

Yes . . . but I found Swiss people very serious.

B

To sound enthusiastic, you should start very high and go down like this:

Yes!

If you are less sure, your voice goes down and then up:

Yes . . .

2  T.4.6.B.  To practise, try first exaggerating, like this:

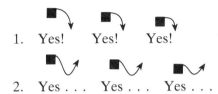

1. Yes!    Yes!    Yes!

2. Yes . . .  Yes . . .  Yes . . .

3  T.4.6.C.  Listen and respond to the questions on the tape, using the prompts below. Decide whether or not you should sound enthusiastic. Pay attention to your intonation of the word *yes*.

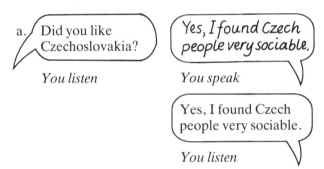

a. Did you like Czechoslovakia?

*You listen*

Yes, I found Czech people very sociable.

*You speak*

Yes, I found Czech people very sociable.

*You listen*

b. **Norway**/helpful

c. **Sweden**/reserved

d. **Australia**/noisy

e. **Italy**/good fun

f. **Brazil**/open

g. **Japan**/quiet

h. **Hungary**/hospitable

# ● Word focus

## 7 Transcribing phonemic script

1  Transcribe these useful words from Unit 4 of the Student's Book.

a. / ʌp'set / _____

b. / 'ædvətaɪz / _____

c. / ə'fensɪv / _____

d. /'vɒləntrɪ / _____

e. / əd'vɜːtɪsmənt / _____

f. / 'lʌgɪdʒ / _____

g. / 'hɪtʃhaɪk / _____

h. / kəm'pleɪn / _____

i. / kə'mɜːʃəl / _____

j. / 'dʒɜːnɪ / _____

k. / 'nɜːvəs / _____

l. / 'vɪəkl / _____

T.4.7.  Listen and practise saying the words.

# ● Everyday English

## 8 Saying the names of countries

1  Do these countries have the same names in your language? Try to guess what the pronunciation is in English.

| | | | |
|---|---|---|---|
| **Egypt** | Iran | **Japan** | Ireland |
| China | **Brazil** | Portugal | |
| **Vietnam** | **Norway** | Poland | Israel |
| Czechoslovakia | | Switzerland | |
| Saudi Arabia | **Belgium** | **Iraq** | |
| **Hungary** | Finland | Canada | |

**T.4.8.A.** Did you guess correctly? Listen and check your answers.

2 Look back, listen again, and mark the stress:

●
Egypt

π—0

3 Practise saying the words, paying attention to the stress.

4 Look at the cities below. They are all in one of the countries in 1. Write where you think each city is.

a. São Paulo *Brazil*

b. Budapest

c. Harbin

d. Faro

e. Baghdad

f. Hanoi

g. Gdansk

h. Jaffa

i. Antwerp

j. Cork

k. Riyadh

5 **T.4.8.B.** Listen and check your answers like this:

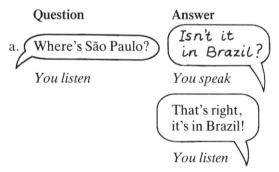

**Question**

a. Where's São Paulo?

*You listen*

**Answer**

Isn't it in Brazil?

*You speak*

That's right, it's in Brazil!

*You listen*

Make sure that you pronounce the names of the countries correctly.

π—0

6 Work in pairs. Ask and answer more questions about different cities. Check in a dictionary the pronunciation of any countries that you are unsure of.

## 9 Saying nationality adjectives

1 Look at the countries in exercise 8 again. What is the adjective for each country?

**Example** *Egypt – Egyptian*

2 Put the adjectives into the right column.

| 1.  -ian | 2.  -ish |
|---|---|
|  |  |

| 3.  -ese | 4.  -i |
|---|---|
|  |  |

| 5.  other |
|---|
|  |

**T.4.9.** Listen and check your answers.

3 Look back, listen again, and mark the stress on each adjective like this ●.

●
**Example** *Egyptian*

Practise saying the words, paying attention to stress.
π—0

4 Can you add any other nationality adjectives to the columns above? Use a dictionary to check where the stress is.

5 For more practice do exercise 6 of this unit.

# UNIT 5

## ● Sounds

### 1 Different pronunciations of '*l*'

1 **T.5.1.A.** A foreign student is practising some of the sentences with '*ll* (*will*) from pages 24 and 25 of the Student's Book. He says some of the sentences correctly, but sometimes he says just *I* instead of *I'll*. Listen and mark the correct sentences *C* and the incorrect sentences *I*.

a. *I*     e. ____

b. ____    f. ____

c. ____    g. ____

d. ____    h. ____

The sound /l/ in *I'll* has a special quality, because it comes at the **end** of the word. This is called **dark** /l/. This is different from an ordinary (clear) /l/.

To make an ordinary /l/, your tongue goes up at the *front* of the mouth like this:

/l/

To make a dark /l/ it **also** goes up at the **back** of the mouth like this:

dark /l/

2 **T.5.1.B.**     If you have problems with the dark /l/ sound, try putting a short /ʊ/ sound between *I* and '*ll*:

I        'll
  /ʊ/

I        'll
  /ʊ/

I        'll
  /ʊ/

3 **T.5.1.C.** Listen and practise saying the sentences correctly.

a. I'll go to the baker's and buy a loaf.
b. I'll go to the post office.
c. I'll buy him a book.
d. I'll buy her a doll.
e. He'll be forty-five next week.
f. I'll have a steak, please.
g. We'll go and visit him.
h. I'll give you my number.

23

4 Write the words from the box next to the name of the shop below where you can buy them.

| | |
|---|---|
| aspirin | shampoo |
| bananas | rolls |
| bread | sausages |
| matches | vodka |
| steak | cigarettes |
| tomatoes | whisky |

**Baker's** _____

**Butcher's** _____

**Chemist's** _____

**Greengrocer's** _____

**Off Licence** _____

**Tobacconist's** _____

🔑━0

5 ┌─────────┐
  │ **T.5.1.D.** │ Listen and respond to A's comment, as
  └─────────┘
in the example:

A ( We haven't got any bread left. )
*You listen*

( Okay, I'll go to the baker's and buy some. )
*You speak*

( Okay, I'll go to the baker's and buy some. )
*You listen*

🔑━0

---

**2** The sounds / ɒ / and / əʊ /
┌──────────────────┐
│ **All Nationalities** │
└──────────────────┘

1 ┌─────────┐
  │ **T.5.2.A.** │ Listen to these two English names, one a
  └─────────┘
man's and one a woman's. Can you hear the
difference between the vowel sounds?

 / ɒ /
John

/ əʊ /
Joan

2 ┌─────────┐
  │ **T.5.2.B.** │ Listen and write in the sounds that you
  └─────────┘
hear – / ɒ / or / əʊ /.

a. ɒ  d. ____  g. ____  j. ____

b. ____  e. ____  h. ____  k. ____

c. ____  f. ____  i. ____  l. ____

🔑━0

3 Practise making the sounds.

/ ɒ / is a short sound. It is made at the back of the
mouth.

/ ɒ /

When you make the sound your lips should look
like this:

/ ɒ /

┌─────────┐
│ **T.5.2.C.** │ Listen and repeat these words:
└─────────┘

| hot | not | shocked | coffee |
|---|---|---|---|
| got | want | modern | yoghurt |

/ əʊ / is a **diphthong** – a long sound made from
putting two vowel sounds together / ə / + / ʊ /. It
starts in the middle of your mouth and moves **back**
and **up** a little. The second sound is very **short**.

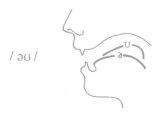

/ əʊ /

When you make the sound your lips should look like this:

/ ə /

/ ʊ /

**T.5.2.D.** Listen and repeat these words:

no        don't      snowing    roll
go        won't      hoping     Poland

4    **T.5.2.E.** Listen to the dialogues and underline all the / ɒ / sounds that you hear.

a.    John! There's Joan on the phone.

Oh no! Not Joan!

b.    It's going to snow!

Oh . . . I won't go home then . . .

No . . .?

c.    Okay then! I'm going!

Oh . . . oh . . . please don't go Polly!

d.    He won't show me those photos, you know!

Why won't he show you them?

I don't know!

Listen again and circle ◯ all the / əʊ / sounds.

π—0

Practise reading the dialogues with a partner. Pay attention to the pronunciation of / ɒ / and / əʊ /.

● **Connected speech**

Do this exercise after the *Weather Forecast* on page 25 of the Student's Book.

**3** Word linking

1    **T.5.3.A.** The weatherman in the weather forecast (page 25 of the Student's Book) speaks very carefully, like most television announcers.

Listen to the first sentence of the weather report again – this time it is read by someone speaking faster and less carefully. Notice the way that the words shown **link together**:

> And now here's the weather forecast for the next twenty-four hours for the whole of England, Wales, Scotland, and Northern Ireland.

With this type of word linking, what sort of sound comes at the beginning of the **second** word?

π—0

2    Here are some more phrases from the weather forecast. How could they be linked in the same way?

> . . . Southern England . . . . . . . . wrap up warm . . .
> . . . Northern Ireland . . . . . . . north easterly winds . . .
> . . . the East coast of England . . .
> . . . the time of year . . .
> . . . the cold front moves in over the Atlantic . . .
> . . . Northern Ireland can expect the same . . .

π—0

**T.5.3.B.** Listen and repeat the phrases paying attention to the word linking.

3    ◀ **T.5.3.A.** This is not the only type of word linking. Listen to the first line of the weather forecast again, and notice how these sounds **disappear** when it is read quickly:

> And now here's the weather forecast for the next twenty-four hours for the whole of England, Wales, Scotland, and Northern Ireland.

What kind of sound comes **before and after** the sound that disappears (except in *Scotland*)?

π—0

4    Here are some more phrases from the weather forecast. Which sounds disappear if you say the phrases quickly?

> . . . the west country . . . . . . . . the East coast . . .
> . . . you can expect some rain . . .
> . . . around the three or four degrees mark . . .
> . . . the highest spots . . . . . . . . the cold front . . .

π—0

**T.5.3.C.** Listen and repeat the phrases, paying attention to the word linking.

5    Work in pairs. Read through the whole of the tapescript of the weather forecast on page 108 of the Student's Book. Decide if there are any more phrases that could be linked together in the ways shown above. Practise reading it aloud.

π—0

25

# ● Intonation and sentence stress

Do this exercise after exercise 7 of this unit.

## 4 Intonation of lists

1 **T.5.4.A.** Listen to the dialogue between the man and the woman. Notice the woman's intonation as she gives the list of things that she wants.

I'm going to the supermarket – do you want anything?

Yes, could you get some yoghurt . . . some mustard . . . and some vinegar.

Does her intonation go **up** or **down** on the words *yoghurt* and *mustard*? What about on the word *vinegar*?

2 **T.5.4.B.** You can practise the intonation by first humming it like this:

. . . de DE-de . . . de  DE-de

de de DE-de-de

. . . some yoghurt . . .

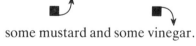

some mustard and some vinegar.

3 Practise the same intonation with the lists below.

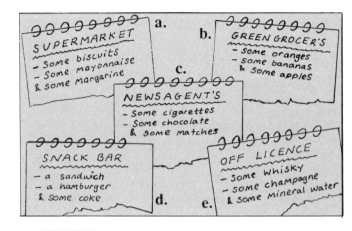

a. **SUPERMARKET**
– Some biscuits
– Some mayonnaise
& some margarine

b. **GREEN GROCER'S**
– Some oranges
– Some bananas
& Some apples

c. **NEWSAGENT'S**
– Some cigarettes
– Some chocolate
& Some matches

d. **SNACK BAR**
– a sandwich
– a hamburger
& Some coke

e. **OFF LICENCE**
– Some whisky
– Some champagne
& Some mineral water

4 **T.5.4.C.** Listen and respond to the questions on the tape following the model in dialogue **T.5.4.A.** Take the woman's part and use the shopping lists above to answer, like this:

a. I'm going to the supermarket – do you want anything?

*You listen*

Yes, could you get some biscuits, some mayonnaise, and some margarine.

*You speak*

Yes, could you get some biscuits, some mayonnaise and some margarine.

*You listen*

## 5 Emphatic stress

1 **T.5.5.** Listen to the dialogue between Sally and her grandfather. Unfortunately her grandfather is deaf – he also worries a lot about what Sally does, and who she meets.

**Sally**  I'm going to meet Ann, grandfather.

**Grandfather**  You're going to meet Sam? Who's Sam?

**Sally**  Not Sam – Ann. We're going to play tennis.

**Grandfather**  You're going to play with Dennis? And who's Dennis?

**Sally**  Not Dennis. Tennis. We're going to play tennis in the park.

**Grandfather**  You're going to play with Dennis and Mark? Who are all these boys you're going to meet?

**Sally**  I'm not going to meet any boys, grandfather. I'm going to play tennis – in the park – with Ann, a girl . . . oh, never mind . . . see you later!

**Grandfather**  Sam . . .? Dennis . . .? Mark . . .? The girl's going mad!

2  Sally and her grandfather **stress** a lot of words very strongly in the conversation. Listen again and mark

the words where the stress is, e.g. *Sam*.

Why do they stress these particular words so strongly?

⌐━0

3  Listen again and read the dialogue together with the tape. You can just mumble the words, like this:

mm MM-mm mm MM MM, MM-mm-mm

I'm going to meet Ann, grandfather.

Pay attention to the stress though.

4  Practise reading the dialogue with a partner, still paying attention to the words that are stressed strongly.

## ● Word focus

Do this exercise after the Vocabulary exercise on page 27 of the Student's Book.

## 6  Adjectives ending in -ed and -ing

1  ⎡ T.5.6. ⎤  You will hear ten different people talking about the topics below. Number the topics in the order that you hear them mentioned.

{ Film      Election results      Divorce }
{ Party 1  Jokes      American      Violinist }
{ Homework      Birthday presents      Baby }

⌐━0

Can you remember anything else that the people said about these topics?

2  Listen to the people again. Which adjectives do they use, one ending in -ed or one ending in -ing? Circle the one that you hear.

a. (disappointed)/disappointing
b. worried/worrying
c. shocked/shocking
d. pleased/pleasing
e. annoyed/annoying
f. excited/exciting
g. interested/interesting
h. amused/amusing
i. disappointed/disappointing
j. bored/boring

⌐━0

## ● Everyday English

## 7  International words for food

1  Look at the words below and tick (✓) the ones that are the same or very similar in your language.

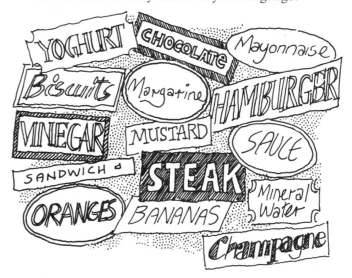

Check the meaning of any words that you do not know.

2  ⎡ T.5.7. ⎤  Try to guess how the words are pronounced in English. Listen and count how many words you guessed correctly.

Listen again and practise saying the words that you guessed wrongly.

# UNIT 6

## ● Sounds

Do this exercise after the Estate Agent's advertisement on pages 31–2 of the Student's Book.

### 1 The sounds / i: / and / ɪ /
Ⓔ Ⓕ Ⓖⓡ Ⓗ Ⓘ Ⓙ Ⓟ Ⓣⓡ

1 ⬚T.6.1.A.⬚ Listen and circle the word that you hear.

  a. (mill)    meal
  b. hills    heels
  c. fill    feel
  d. pitch    peach
  e. slip    sleep
  f. will    wheel

π—0

2 Practise making the sounds.

You should smile, and your mouth should be slightly open to make the sound / i: /. Your tongue should be forward and up in your mouth, too. / i: / is a **long** sound.

/ i: /

You should open your mouth a little more, and move your tongue down a bit, to make the sound / ɪ /. / ɪ / is a **short** sound.

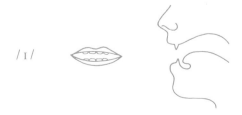

/ ɪ /

3 ⬚T.6.1.B.⬚ Listen to these pairs of words and repeat them.

| / i: / | / ɪ / |
| --- | --- |
| wheel | will |
| feel | fill |
| meal | mill |
| peach | pitch |
| heel | hill |
| sleep | slip |

4 All the words below come from the Estate Agent's advertisements on pages 31 and 32 of the Student's Book. Can you remember what they all mean?

     /i:/
  a. cl<u>ea</u>n        g. kitchen

  b. detached     h. living room

  c. convenient   i. minutes

  d. cottage      j. peace

  e. description   k. reception room

  f. dream       l. residential street

⬚T.6.1.C.⬚ All of the words and phrases contain either the sound / ɪ / or the sound / i: / or both. Listen and mark them / ɪ / or / i:/.

π—0

Listen again and practise saying the words correctly.

Do this exercise after Language Review 2 on page 32 of the Student's Book.

## 2 The pronunciation of *-er* and *-est* at the end of words

1 | **T.6.2.A.** | Listen to these adjectives, comparatives and superlatives. How are *-er* and *-est* pronounced?

| | | |
|---|---|---|
| big | bigger | biggest |
| cheap | cheaper | cheapest |
| slim | slimmer | slimmest |
| deep | deeper | deepest |
| clean | cleaner | cleanest |
| rich | richer | richest |
| easy | easier | easiest |
| pretty | prettier | prettiest |

2 Listen and repeat the adjectives.

3 Read the questions and circle the correct answer.

a. Which building is the oldest?
 *The Taj Mahal   The Parthenon*
 *The Colosseum*

b. Which city is the biggest?
 *London   Tokyo   Mexico City*

c. Which country is the smallest?
 *Monaco   Luxemburg   Hungary*

d. Which animal is the fastest?
 *the lion   the cheetah   the tiger*

e. Which lake is the deepest?
 *Loch Ness   Lake Michigan   Lake Baikal*

f. Which bridge is the newest?
 *Tower Bridge   The Golden Gate Bridge*
 *The Bridge of Sighs*

g. Which monument is the tallest?
 *The Eiffel Tower   The Statue of Liberty*
 *Nelson's Column*

h. Which river is the longest?
 *The Mississippi   The Nile   The Danube*

i. Which mountain is the highest?
 *Mont Blanc   Mount Fuji   Mount Everest*

j. Which planet is the largest?
 *Mars   Jupiter   Venus*

4 | **T.6.2.B.** | Listen and respond like this:

| Question | Answer |
|---|---|
| a. Which building is the oldest – the Taj Mahal, the Parthenon or the Colosseum? | *The Parthenon's the oldest, isn't it?* |
| *You listen* | *You speak* |
| | That's right, the Parthenon's the oldest. |
| | *You listen* |

How many did you get wrong?

## 3 The sounds / s / and / ʃ /

Ⓔ Ⓖⓡ Ⓙ

1   **T.6.3.A.**   Listen and circle the word that you hear.

   a. (sure)      sore
   b. ship        sip
   c. sheet       seat
   d. shaved      saved
   e. shoot       suit

   π—0

2   Practise making the sounds.

   Your tongue should be forward in your mouth to
   make the sound / s /.

   / s /

   To make the sound / ʃ / you should move your
   tongue back and up a little in your mouth.

   / ʃ /

   Both / s / and / ʃ / are **voiceless**.

3   **T.6.3.B.**   Listen to these words and repeat them.

   / s /     / ʃ /
   sea       she
   seat      sheet
   sore      sure
   save      shave
   sip       ship
   suit      shoot
   sell      shell

4   Work with a partner. You say a word and your
   partner listens and points to the word he or she
   hears.

5   Learn this rhyme by heart:

   *She sells sea shells on the seashore.*
   *And the shells that she sells*
   *Are sea shells, I'm sure.*

   Practise saying it as fast as you can.

Do this exercise after the poem *Warning* on page 34
of the Student's Book.

## 4 / s /, / z / or / ʃ /?

**All Nationalities**

1   These words all come from the poem *Warning* on
   page 34 of the Student's Book.

   Put them into the correct columns, according to the
   sound (or sounds) that they contain.

   | | | |
   |---|---|---|
   | shall | slippers | shock |
   | doesn't | pounds | pencils |
   | pension | us | surprised |
   | gloves | practise | clothes |
   | press | sausages | start |

   | / s / | / z / |
   |---|---|
   |  |  |
   |  |  |
   |  |  |

   | / s / and / z / | / ʃ / |
   |---|---|
   |  |  |
   |  |  |

   π—0

2   Check the pronunciation of any new words in a
   dictionary. Practise saying them.

   Can you find any more words in the poem with
   these sounds in them?

3   Practise reading the poem aloud, paying attention
   to these sounds.

## ● Connected speech

## 5 *As . . . as* – weak forms and word linking

a picture

a feather

a peacock

a bat

a church mouse

a post

1 Finish these English sayings using one of the words in the pictures.

She's as pretty as _____

He's as poor as _____

He's as proud as _____

She's as deaf as _____

It's as light as _____

She's as blind as _____

**T.6.5.** Listen and check your answers.

Which words in each sentence are *stressed*?

How is the word *as* pronounced?

Notice how the words link together when the sentences are said quickly.

She's as pretty as a picture.

2 Look at the other sentences again. How could they link together in the same way?

3 Listen and repeat the sentences. Pay attention to the pronunciation of *as* and the word linking.

4 Do you have any idioms similar to this in your language? How would they translate into English?

## ● Intonation and sentence stress

## 6 Showing degrees of enthusiasm

We can show how enthusiastic we are through the words we use.

*    He's *quite nice*.    (not very enthusiastic)
**    He's *nice*.    (more enthusiastic)
***    He's *really nice*.    (very enthusiastic)

When speaking, we don't always change the words we use. We can show how enthusiastic we are through **intonation**.

1    **T.6.6.**    Listen to the first three dialogues below and make sure that you can hear the difference in degrees of enthusiasm.

Now listen to the rest of the dialogue and mark them * (not very enthusiastic) ** (more enthusiastic) or *** (most enthusiastic).

a. **Q** What was the film like?
   **A** Mmm. It was good.    ✳

b. **Q** What was the meal like?
   **A** Mmm. It was good.    ✳ ✳

c. **Q** What was the weather like?
   **A** Mmm. It was good.    ✳✳✳

d. **Q** What's Sandra like?
   **A** Oh, she's nice.

e. **Q** What's Sue like?
   **A** Oh, she's nice.

f. **Q** What's Mrs Smith like?
   **A** Oh, she's nice.

g. **Q** What was the play like?
   **A** It was interesting.

h. **Q** What was the tour like?
   **A** It was interesting.

i. **Q** What was the town like?
   **A** It was interesting.

2 Listen again and try to copy the intonation.

# 7 Shifting stress

1 **T.6.7.A.** Listen to the short dialogues below. In B's answer one word is stressed more strongly than the others. Mark the word like this ■.

a. **A** *Is she thin, grey-haired, and in her forties?*

   **B** *No, she's fat, grey-haired, and in her forties.*

b. **A** *Is she thin, grey-haired, and in her forties?*

   **B** *No, she's thin, red-haired, and in her forties.*

c. **A** *Is she thin, grey-haired, and in her forties?*

   **B** *No, she's thin, grey-haired, and in her fifties.*

Is it always the same word that is stressed in **B**'s answer?

In each dialogue, why has **B** stressed this particular word so strongly?

2 Listen, and practise reading **B**'s part aloud.

Make sure you put the stress in the right part of the sentence.

3 **T.6.7.B.** Look at the answers below. Each one has the stress marked in a different place. Listen to the questions, and put a tick (√) next to the correct answer, according to the stress.

a. 1. No, he's got ■short, dark, straight hair.

   2. No, he's got short, ■dark, straight hair.

   3. No, he's got short, dark, ■straight hair.  √

b. 1. No, ■Helen was the one in her late thirties.

   2. No, Helen was the one in her ■late thirties.

   3. No, Helen was the one in her late ■thirties.

c. 1. No, it's a ■modern red-brick house.

   2. No, it's a modern ■red-brick house.

   3. No, it's a modern red-■brick house.

d. 1. No, he's ■mad about playing football.

   2. No, he's mad about ■playing football.

   3. No, he's mad about playing ■football.

e. 1. No, he's ■young, rich, and stupid.

   2. No, he's young, ■rich, and stupid.

   3. No, he's young, rich, and ■stupid.

f. 1. No, she's got a ■stomach ache, a sore throat, and a temperature.

   2. No, she's got a stomach ache, a sore ■throat, and a temperature.

   3. No, she's got a stomach ache, a sore throat, and a ■temperature.

4 Listen again, and reply to the questions.

Make sure you put the stress in the right part of the sentence.

# ● Word focus

Do this exercise after the Vocabulary exercise on page 33 of the Student's Book.

## 8 Phonemic transcription

1   The words below are all adjectives for describing people. Can you transcribe them?

   a.  / ə'dɔːrəbl /  _____

   b.  / 'tʃɪəfl /  _____

   c.  / ɪŋ'kwɪzɪtɪv /  _____

   d.  / 'pʌŋktʃʊəl /  _____

   e.  / rɪ'laɪəbl /  _____

   f.  / 'selfɪʃ /  _____

   g.  / 'sensətɪv /  _____

   h.  / 'səʊʃəbl /  _____

   i.  / spɒn'teɪnɪəs /  _____

   j.  / 'tæktfl /  _____

   k.  / 'tɒlərənt /  _____

   l.  / 'wɪtɪ /  _____

2   Use the phonemic transcription to mark the stress. Work out how to say the words.

   ㅠ—0

3   **T.6.8.**  Listen and check your answers.

# ● Everyday English

## 9 Saying punctuation marks

1   Write the names next to these punctuation marks.

   | apostrophe | exclamation mark |
   |---|---|
   | full stop | inverted commas |
   | comma | question mark |

   a.  •  _____

   b.  ,  _____

   c.  ,  _____

   d.  ' ,  _____

   e.  ?  _____

   f.  !  _____

2   **T.6.9.A.**  Listen to check your answers. Practise saying the words.

3   **T.6.9.B.**  Listen to the tape. You will be given instructions as to how to punctuate the following sentences. Follow the instructions. You will need to add some capital letters yourself.

   a.  you pig mary jane said angrily

   _____

   b.  john my brother who lives in oxford loves fishing

   _____

   c.  he left his students english homework in a taxi

   _____

   d.  is your birthday in february april asked david

   ㅠ—0

# UNIT 7

## ● Sounds

---

**1 The sounds / æ / and / ʌ /**
Ⓔ Ⓕ Ⓖⓡ Ⓘ Ⓙ Ⓟ Ⓣⓡ

1 Write in the Past Simple and Past Participle of the verbs below.

a. run _____ _____

b. sing _____ _____

c. ring _____ _____

d. swim _____ _____

e. begin _____ _____

f. drink _____ _____

2 **T.7.1.A.** Can you hear the difference between the Past Simple (spelt with *a*) and the Past Participle (spelt with *u*)?

/ æ / / ʌ /
ran run

3 **T.7.1.B.** Look back at 1 above. Listen and circle the verb that you hear – Past Simple or Past Participle.

**Example** (ran) run

To make the sound / æ / your mouth should be open like this, and your tongue should be down at the front of your mouth:

/ æ /

To make the sound / ʌ / your mouth should be less open and your tongue should be a little higher in your mouth:

/ ʌ /

4 Of course in a sentence, you can also tell from the grammar if it is the Past Simple or the Past Participle. Put the sentences below into the correct tense.

a. ☐ I̶ Look! the children ~~drank~~ / *have drunk* everything.

b. ☐ C Her boyfriend *rang* / *has rung* her eight times yesterday.

c. ☐ C I'm sorry you can't go into the theatre – the play *already began* / *has already begun*.

d. ☐ I I *just swam* / *have just swum* a kilometre.

e. ☐ C I don't feel very well – I *drank* / *have drunk* ten whiskies last night.

f. ☐ I My legs hurt – I *ran* / *have run* ten miles yesterday.

5 | **T.7.1.C.** | Now listen to the student who is reading them aloud. Look back at point 4 and mark the box on the left _C_ if the verb is pronounced correctly and _I_ if the verb is pronounced incorrectly.

Practise saying the sentences correctly yourself.

---

## 2 The sound / h /
(E) (F) (Gr) (I) (P)

To make the sound / h / you should push a lot of air out of your mouth without moving your tongue. The sound is similar to the noise you make if you are out of breath.

/ h /

1 | **T.7.2.A.** | Listen and practise saying these words.

| | | |
|---|---|---|
| Hi | home | hitch-hike |
| Hello | holiday | farmhouse |
| have | hotel | comprehension |

2 | **T.7.2.B.** | Listen to the sentences below and underline ____ the / h / sounds that you hear.

a. Helen has cut her own hair again – it's absolutely horrible!

b. Have you heard about Hanna's horrific adventure in Hamburg?

c. Henry's Uncle Herbert has had another heart attack in hospital.

d. Old Hugh hasn't eaten his ham and eggs already, has he?

e. Hazel and Alan have had another unhappy holiday hitch-hiking in Austria and Hungary.

There are six words where the letter _h_ is not pronounced. Go back and cross out these _h_s, like this: ✗.

What sort of words have silent _h_s? Why do you think the _h_ is silent?

3 Practise saying each of the sentences in 2 five times. Start by saying it very slowly, and gradually say it faster and faster. Pay attention to the / h / sounds. Be careful not to put in any extra / h / sounds.

4 Look at the words below. Seven of them are 'exceptions'. They are not weak forms but the _h_ at the beginning of the syllable is not pronounced. Use a dictionary to find the seven words. At the same time you can check the meaning of any words that you do not know.

| | | |
|---|---|---|
| hole | whole | ghost |
| behind | vehicle | exhibition |
| hour | who | how |
| rehearse | childhood | honest |
| heir | inherit | dishonest |

Close your book. Can you remember the seven words where _h_ is not pronounced?

## ● Connected speech

---

### 3 The weak forms of _for_

When the word _for_ comes in the middle of a phrase or sentence, it is not pronounced / fɔ: /, but either / fə / or / fər /.

1 | **T.7.3.A.** | Listen to these expressions with _for_ and put them into the correct column.

| / fə / | / fər / |
|---|---|
| _for ten years_ | |

2 What is the difference between the expressions with / fə / and the expressions with / fər /?

Why do we pronounce the / r / in the second case do you think?

Practise saying the expressions correctly. With the expressions in column 2 link the / r / sound onto the beginning of the next word like this:

for a week or two.

3  **T.7.3.B.**  Listen and answer the questions on the tape using the prompts below, like this:

a. *fourteen years*

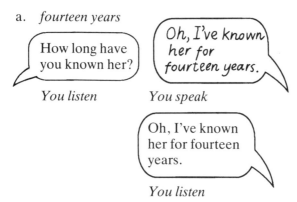

How long have you known her?

*You listen*

Oh, I've known her for fourteen years.

*You speak*

Oh, I've known her for fourteen years.

*You listen*

b. *for ages and ages*
c. *for a couple of months*
d. *for four or five days*
e. *for twenty-five years*
f. *for a fortnight*
g. *for about two years*
h. *for the whole summer*
i. *for a few minutes*

Pay attention to your pronunciation of *for*.

---

## 4  Strong and weak forms of auxiliary verbs – revision

1  **T.7.4.A.**  Listen to the short dialogues below. Mark the auxiliary verb *S* if it is strong and *w* if it is weak.

a.  A  Dave *was* sleeping when I got in!  w
    B  *Was* he?                            S

b.  A  *Do* you enjoy cooking?
    B  Yes, actually, I *do*.

c.  A  *Shall* we go out for lunch?
    B  Mmm . . . *shall* we?

d.  A  *Has* he been ill again?
    B  Yes, I'm afraid he *has*.

e.  A  We *were* walking past when it happened.
    B  *Were* you really?

f.  A  *Have* they been away?
    B  I think they *have*.

g.  A  *Can* you play the guitar, Sally?
    B  Mmm . . . I *can* a bit . . .

When are the auxiliary verbs **weak**? When are they **strong**? What is the vowel sound in all the weak forms?

2  Listen again and repeat the dialogues. Pay attention to the strong and weak forms.

3  **T.7.4.B.**  Listen to the dialogue below and read as you listen. Check the meaning of any new words.

A  *Have* you ever been to Ireland, Pete?
B  Yes, loads of times. My parents go over there every year, you see.
A  *Do* they? Why's that then?
B  Oh, my Dad *was* born in Dublin.
A  *Was* he really? He doesn't sound Irish at all!
B  No . . . well his family left when he *was* about ten. What about you? *Have* you ever been over there?
A  Well, we *were* going to Dublin last summer and then there *was* that long ferry strike . . .
B  That's right, there *was*.
A  Anyway we *were* hoping to go this year instead, but hotel prices *have* gone up so much . . .
B  Yes, I know they *have*, it's terrible. I tell you what, *shall* I give you my cousin's address? Perhaps you *can* stay with her for a few days?
A  Are you sure we *can*? It seems a bit cheeky . . .
B  No . . .

4  Read the dialogue again and look at the auxiliary verbs in italics. If you think the strong form is used underline the verb like this _____ , if you think the weak form is used, underline like this ∿∿∿ .

Listen and check your answers.

5  Practise reading the dialogue with a partner. Pay attention to the weak and strong forms of auxiliary verbs.

# ● Intonation

## 5 Question tags with falling intonation

1 **T.7.5.A.** Steve is applying for the job of chief computer programmer at ABC Computers. Margaret Peters is interviewing him. Listen and complete their dialogue.

> You _____ to Manchester University _____ ?

> Yes _____ right.

> But you _____ in Canada for _____ _____ years, _____ ?

> Yes, I _____

2 Look at what Margaret says again. Do you think she already knows these facts about Steve or not?

These questions at the end of the sentences are called **question tags**. In this dialogue the question tags go **down** at the end, because Margaret already knows the answer to the question – she is just using the question tag to **check the information**.

Notice that the sentences are **affirmative**, but the question tags are **negative**.

When is *haven't you?* used? When is *didn't you?* used?

3 **T.7.5.B.** You can practise the intonation by first exaggerating like this:

Didn't you?    Didn't you?    Didn't you?

You went to Manchester University, didn't you?

Haven't you?    Haven't you?    Haven't you?

You've been in Canada for the last ten years, haven't you?

4 Here are some more things that Margaret says. Complete the sentences with *didn't you?* and *haven't you?*.

a. You studied computer science at university, _____ ?
b. You finished your degree in 1977, _____ ?
c. You've worked for Banana Computers since then, _____ ?
d. You went to Canada in 1979, _____ ?
e. You've also worked in Australia _____ ?
f. You met your wife in Australia, _____ ?
g. You've been married for five years, _____ ?
h. You and your wife have just had a baby, _____ ?

5 **T.7.5.C.** Listen and take the part of Margaret, using the sentences above.

a. You studied computer science at university, didn't you?

*You speak*

You studied computer science at university, didn't you?

*You listen*

Yes, that's right.

*You listen*

## ● Word focus

Do this exercise after the dialogue on page 37 of the Student's Book.

## 6 Words that begin with 'a'

1   On page 37 of the Student's Book there are 10 words **of more than one syllable** beginning with *a*. Find them and check the pronunciation in the dictionary. Put them into the correct column below, according to how the *a* is pronounced. Remember to mark the stress.

| / ə / | / æ / |
|---|---|
|  |  |

| / eɪ / | / eə / |
|---|---|
|  |  |

| / ɑː / |
|---|
|  |

π—0

2   What do you notice about the stress on the words beginning with the sound / ə /?

What about the stress in the other words?

π—0
Practise saying the words correctly.

3   | T.7.6. |   Here are some more words beginning with *a*. Listen and put them into the correct column opposite.

| America | Africa | amusing | agree |
|---|---|---|---|
| accent | attractive | Asia | able |
| around | about | ago | alone |
| aeroplane | Atlantic | arrive |  |

π—0
Can you think of any other words to put in these columns?

4   Try to remember how the *a* is pronounced at the beginning of each of the words in the columns and then make sentences using the words. Try to use as many of the words as you can in each sentence:

**Example**   She went *abroad about* seven years *ago*. *Actually*, I think she's got a very *attractive accent*.

Practise saying your sentences aloud.

## ● Everyday English

## 7 Saying dates – years

1   Below are some important facts about British history. Read them and make sure that you understand all the words. Do you know any of the missing dates?

a.   England and Scotland have had the same king since _____ .

b.   Britain hasn't governed the United States since _____ .

c.   Women in Britain have had the vote since _____ .

d.   Elizabeth II has been Queen since _____ .

e.   England hasn't been successfully invaded since _____ .

f.   Britain hasn't governed India since _____ .

g.   Britain has been a member of the European Community since _____ .

h.   Britain hasn't had a successful revolution since _____ .

2    **T.7.7.A.** Listen and write in the dates that you do not know.

3    **T.7.7.B.** Notice the stress pattern when you say dates like this in English:

☐ sixteen o-three

☐ seventeen seventy-six

☐ nineteen nineteen

Listen again and practise saying the sentences in 1.

4    Write down ten important dates in the history of your country and practise saying them. Compare your list with a partner. Which do you think are the most important dates of all?

# 8 Revision of numbers, dates, and spelling

1    You will hear a woman telephoning a travel agent's to book a flight to Madrid from London. First check that you understand the words below. How are they pronounced?

> reduction       reservation
> full fare        flight number

2    **T.7.8.** Listen to the dialogue and fill in the gaps. You will probably need to listen more than once.

TA  Hello, Pentagon Travel.
C   Hello, I'd like to fly return to Madrid. Can you tell me how much it would cost?
TA  When would you like to travel?
C   I'd like to go on Sunday, the (a.)

_____ and come back on Friday, the

(b.) _____ .
TA  Well . . . I'm afraid you'll have to pay full fare

then . . . that's . . . (c.) _____ return.
C   As much as that!
TA  You can't wait and come back on the thirtieth?
C   Does that make a difference?
TA  Yes, you can get a special reduction if you stay for seven days – it would only be (d.)

_____ .
C   Oh, that's quite a big difference, isn't it? I'll do that, then. Can you give me the times and the flight numbers?
TA  Yes, on the way there you leave London

Heathrow at (e.) _____ and arrive in Madrid

at (f.) _____ . The flight number's (g.)

_____ .
C   And coming back?
TA  You come back in the afternoon – you leave

Madrid at 16.20 – that's (h.) _____ and arrive

back at Heathrow at 18.10 – that's (i.) _____ .
    Shall I make a reservation then, Madam?
C   Yes, please. My name's Susan (j.) _____ –
    that's (k.) _____ .
TA  Thank you. And could I have your address and telephone number too, please?
C   Yes, it's 10 (l.) _____ Avenue . . .
TA  How do you spell that?
C   (m.) _____ . It's London (n.) _____ . The

phone number's (o.) _____ .
TA  Right, thanks a lot. Remember, you should pay before the 15th of September.
C   Fine . . . thank you for your help. Goodbye.
TA  Goodbye.
C   Fine . . . thank you for your help. Goodbye.
TA  Goodbye.

3    Listen again and read the dialogue at the same time as the tape. Practise until you are happy with your pronunciation.

4    Practise reading the dialogue with a partner. Now make up similar dialogues about flights from your country to other cities – for example, Amsterdam, New York, Milan.

# UNIT 8

## ● Sounds

### 1 The sound / ɜː /

Vowels spelt with *ir*, *or*, *er*, *ur*, or *ear* are often pronounced / ɜː /:

| /ɜː/ | /ɜː/ | /ɜː/ |
|------|------|------|
| sh<u>ir</u>t | w<u>or</u>d | p<u>er</u>son |
| | /ɜː/ | /ɜː/ |
| | f<u>ur</u>ther | <u>ear</u>l |

1 **T.8.1.A.** Listen to these groups of words and circle the one that is *not* pronounced / ɜː /:

a. girl (tired) bird first

b. worm worn world work

c. adv<u>er</u>tisement univ<u>er</u>sity cons<u>er</u>vative west<u>er</u>n

d. n<u>ur</u>se b<u>ur</u>y sub<u>ur</u>b dist<u>ur</u>b

e. learn earn wear earl

To make the sound / ɜː / your lips and tongue should be in the same position as to make the sound / ə /, but / ɜː / is *longer*:

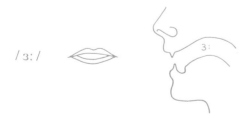

2 Listen again and practise saying the words correctly.

3 Read the following dialogue and underline all the syllables which you think are pronounced with an / ɜː / sound.

**A** Are all your friends from university working now?

**B** Nearly. Kirsty's doing research work at Birmingham University and Shirley's gone to work as a nurse in the Third World – Burma or somewhere.

**A** Really? That's adventurous. What about Pearl?

**B** Oh, Pearl's turned really conservative. She's a civil servant now. She and Kirk live in some suburb somewhere.

**A** And how about Dirk?

**B** Oh, haven't you heard about Dirk? He's working in Turkey as a windsurf instructor! He's learnt Turkish and he's earning a fortune . . . or so I've heard.

**T.8.1.B.** Listen and check your answers.

4 Listen again and repeat the dialogue.

Practise reading the dialogue with a partner.

# ● Connected speech

## 2 Word linking – sound changes

The reading on pages 44–45 of the Student's Book is about the *London Marathon* and the Sunday Times Fun Run in *Hyde Park*. Notice that when these two expressions are said quickly, the consonant sound at the end of the first word can change:

/m/ London Marathon    /b/ Hyde Park

1 **T.8.2.A.** Listen to the names of some London Underground Stations below. How does the consonant sound at the end of the first word in each name change when the names are said quickly?

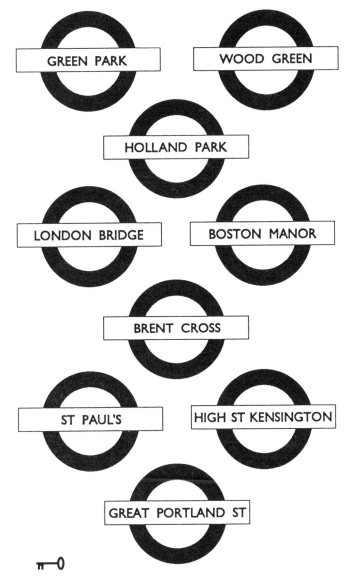

2 Listen again and practise saying the names quickly with the sound changes.

3 Sound changes are not the only type of word linking. Can you remember any other types? How could the names below be linked together if they were said quickly?

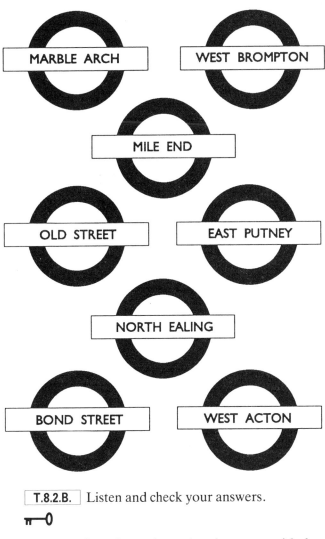

**T.8.2.B.** Listen and check your answers.

🗝—0

4 Listen again and practise saying the names with the word linking.

## 3 Modals of obligation in connected speech

1 **T.8.3.** Listen and write in the box on the left the number of words you hear in the sentence (*haven't* is **two** words).

a. ☐ I _____
tell _____ it .

b. ☐ I _____
it _____ .

c. ☐ _____
tell me .

d. ☐ _____
work _____ hard .

e. ☐ _____
go _____ already?

f. ☐ _____
be _____ nine .

g. ☐ _____ mustn't
_____ late _____ .

h. ☐ _____
think I _____ ?

i. ☐ I _____
_____ worry .

Listen again and fill in the missing words.

2 What do you notice about the pronunciation of *must*?

Is *should* stressed or not?

What sound change do you notice in *have to*? What about in *has to*?

Listen again and repeat the sentences, paying attention to stress, weak forms and the sound changes mentioned above.

## ● Intonation and sentence stress

## 4 Giving advice politely

1 **T.8.4.A.** Emma has got hiccups. Listen to the advice her friend gives her and fill in the missing words. You will hear the intonation pattern first in each case.

*Should* is very often used to give advice and make suggestions in English. To sound polite your voice should go high on the first stressed word in the sentence and then down on the last stressed word:

You should hold your breath.

Remember, *should* is **not** usually stressed unless you want to give strong emphasis to the suggestion.

◀ **T.8.4.A.** Practise the intonation. Try first humming like this:

de   de   DE   de   DE . . .

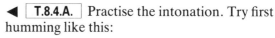

You should hold your breath.

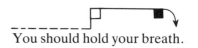

de   de   DE de DE de DE-de . . .

You should drink a glass of water.

de   de   DE de de-de DE-de de . . .

You should take a little lemon juice.

Remember that if your intonation is flat, you will probably sound impolite.

3 T.8.4.B. Listen to some people complaining and give them advice using the picture prompts below, like this:

a. I've got a terrible cold!

*You listen*

You should go to bed.

*You speak*

You should go to bed.

*You listen*

π—O

Do this exercise after the writing exercise on page 47 of the Student's Book.

## 5 Reading aloud

1 T.8.5.A. Listen to the first paragraph of the writing exercise and mark the stressed syllables with a box: □

□ □ □ □ □
Doing regular exercise can be dangerous, especially

□ □
if you are over forty. This is why it is a very good

idea to see your doctor before starting if you think

you are not very fit. Some people try to exercise too

vigorously too soon, and as a result they cause

themselves injuries which can take a long time to

heal.

π—O

2 What kind of words, generally, are stressed?

What kind of words are not stressed? What happens to many of these words?

π—O

◄ T.8.5.A. Listen again and read along with the tape **mumbling** the words, but paying attention to stress and rhythm:

□ □ □
MM-mm MM-mm-mm MM-mm-mm mm mm

□ □
MM-mm-mm, mm-MM-mm-mm mm mm mm

□ □
MM-mm MM-mm

T.8.5.B. Practise some of the phrases, paying attention to the stress and weak forms. Start at the end of the phrase, like this:

□
dangerous
be dangerous
can be dangerous
doing regular exercise can be dangerous

□ □
over forty
are over forty
you are over forty
if you are over forty

◄ T.8.5.A. Listen to the whole paragraph again and read along with the tape until you are satisfied with your pronunciation. Now look at the **second** paragraph of the exercise on page 47 of the Student's Book and try to read it in the same way – paying attention to stress and weak forms.

## ● Word focus

Do this exercise after the reading on page 45 of the Student's Book.

## 6 Nouns ending in -ness and adjectives ending in -less

Many nouns in English are made by adding -ness to the adjective:

ill-*ness*    tired-*ness*
fit-*ness*    sore-*ness*

This is pronounced / nəs /.

1   Here are 20 more adjectives, but only 15 of them have nouns made with -ness. Can you find the five which *don't*?

| | |
|---|---|
| kind | weak |
| young | selfish |
| polite | lazy |
| sweet | cheerful |
| mean | beautiful |
| rude | ugly |
| friendly | thin |
| energetic | old |
| shy | happy |
| strong | sad |

**T.8.6.**   Listen and check to see if you were right. You will hear **only** the words which take -*ness*.

What are the nouns for the other five words?

⚓—O

2   Listen again and practise saying the words, paying attention to the pronunciation of -*ness*.

Can you think of any more nouns ending in -*ness*?

3   Try to guess how -*less* is pronounced at the end of these adjectives:

| | |
|---|---|
| breathless | useless |
| careless | tactless |

Can you think of any more adjectives like this?

⚓—O

## 7 Words related to health

1   Make sure that you can remember what all the words in the left column mean. If you cannot, check them in the dictionary.

2   Match up the words on the left with their phonemic spelling on the right. Then refer to phonemic transcription to mark the stress, like this:

●
treatment        / ˈeɪkɪŋ /

poison           / sɔː /

breathe          / breθ /

breath           / ˈbændɪdʒ /

injury           / helθ /

muscle           / ˈswəʊlən /

aching           / ˈtriːtmənt /

health           / hiːl /

heal             / bruːz /

heart            / briːð /

sprained         / ˈmʌsl /

swollen          / hɑːt /

sore             / ˈɪndʒərɪ /

bruise           / spreɪnd /

bandage          / ˈpɔɪzən /

⚓—O

3   **T.8.7.**   Practise saying the words. Listen and check your pronunciation.

How many words did you get wrong? Listen to these words again and practise saying them correctly.

44

## 8 International words – illnesses

1 Which of the words below are the same or very similar in your language? Look up any that you do not understand in your dictionary.

> bronchitis      diabetes
> tonsilitis       influenza (flu)
> appendicitis     cancer
> hepatitis        rheumatism
> anaemia          diarrhoea
> AIDS             malaria

2 **T.8.8.** Try to guess how they are pronounced in English and then listen to see how many you guessed correctly.

Listen again and practise saying the words that you guessed incorrectly.

3 Work with a partner. Discuss the answers to the following questions. Pay attention to your pronunciation.

Which of the illnesses above are the least serious, do you think?
Which ones usually affect old people?
Which ones might require an operation?
Which ones are conditions that might last for one's whole lifetime?

## ● Everyday English

## 9 Saying fractions and decimals

1 **T.8.9.A.** Listen to the different ways that fractions and decimals are pronounced in English. Repeat the phrases.

½  ¼  ⅕  ⅔  ⁵⁄₁₂

.1  .5  .75  .285  .07

2 **T.8.9.B.** Listen and answer the questions like this:

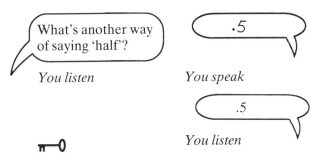

> What's another way of saying 'half'?

*You listen*

> .5

*You speak*

> .5

*You listen*

3 Ask your partner some more questions like those in 9.2 above.

4 How do you think we say these numbers in English?

> 26.2    2.5    2.2    4.53
> 99.9    33.3   20.05  11.995

5 Work in pairs. One of you is **A**; one of you is **B**. **A** should close his or her book and **B** should read out the questions. **A** must not look at **B**'s book. The first pair in the class to finish all the questions should shout 'Stop!' and the rest of the class should then stop asking questions.

a. What is normal human body temperature in degrees centigrade?
   (i) *36.8*
   (ii) *38.6*
   (iii) *37*

b. What is the mathematical number *pi*?
   (i) *3.41*
   (ii) *3.14*
   (iii) *4.13*

c. In the 1984 Olympics, what was the record in the men's 100 metres?
   (i) *9.09 seconds*
   (ii) *9.99 seconds*
   (iii) *10.09 seconds*

d. In the same Olympics, what was the record in the women's 100 metres?
   (i) *10.97 seconds*
   (ii) *9.97 seconds*
   (iii) *11.97 seconds*

e. How many litres are there in a pint?
   (i) *0.586*
   (ii) *0.856*
   (iii) *0.732*

f. How many pounds are there in a kilo?
   (i) *1.8*
   (ii) *2.5*
   (iii) *2.2*

g. How many centimetres are there in an inch?
   (i) *2.05*
   (ii) *2.54*
   (iii) *2.45*

h. Approximately how many kilometres are there in a mile?
   (i) *1.5*
   (ii) *1.6*
   (iii) *1.7*

Who got the most correct answers in the class?

# UNIT 9

## ● Sounds

### 1 The sounds / ʃ / and / tʃ /
Ⓓ Ⓔ Ⓕ Ⓖⓡ Ⓘ

1 **T.9.1.A.** Listen to the following pairs of words and make sure that you can hear the difference between the sounds / ʃ / and / tʃ /.

a. (sherry)  cherry    d. shops  chops
b. shin      chin       e. dish   ditch
c. ships    chips     f. wash  watch

2 **T.9.1.B.** Listen and circle the word above that you hear in each sentence.

To make the sound / ʃ / the tongue should be raised in the middle of the mouth. It is the sound that we make when we want someone to be quiet.

/ tʃ / is a combination of / t / and / ʃ /.

Try saying the two sounds separately, / t / then / ʃ /. Keep repeating them more quickly each time until you say them together.

You do **not** use your voice to make the sounds / ʃ / or / tʃ /.

3 Listen to the pairs of words in **T.9.1.A.** again and repeat, paying attention to the pronunciation of the two different sounds.

4 **T.9.1.C.** Check the meaning of any of the words below that you do not know. Listen and practise saying the words.

| | | |
|---|---|---|
| portion | cherry cheesecake | kitchen shelf |
| Czech | chewed | checked shorts |
| merchant | purchased | shining Porsche |
| chess | chase | chambermaid |

5 **T.9.1.D.** Now listen to these tongue-twisters and underline all the / ʃ / sounds that you hear like this ____ .

a. Which of Shirley Hatchard's children stole a portion of cherry cheesecake from the kitchen shelf?
b. Sheila Charlton's Czech washing machine chewed up Richard Sheridan's checked shorts.
c. The rich Turkish sugar merchant purchased a shining Porsche for his Chinese chauffeur to polish.
d. Sasha, the Russian chess champion, chased Sharon, the Scottish chambermaid, round the kitchen floor, so Sharon showed Sasha the door.

Listen again and underline like this 〰〰 all the / tʃ / sounds that you hear.

6 Practise saying the tongue-twisters five times each. Start by saying them slowly and then say them faster and faster.

46

# ● Connected speech

## 2 Contractions of *will* and *would*

1  **T.9.2.A.** Listen to the mini-dialogues and write **1** in the box if the answer to the question is in the **first** conditional and **2** in the box if the answer is in the **second** conditional. Listen only once and do not stop the tape.

a. I'm so busy I don't know what to do.

Don't worry, I (help) you if you (want).  `1`

b. Why haven't you been jogging today?

I (go) if it (be) a bit sunnier.  ☐

c. Why don't you ever do any work in this office?

I (work) harder if you (pay) me more!  ☐

d. Why are you so quiet? What's the matter?

You (be) angry, if I (tell) you . . .  ☐

e. What are you doing this evening, Joe?

I think I (stay) in if there (be) anything good on television.  ☐

f. Why haven't my parents phoned?

If there (be) a problem, they (phone).  ☐

g. Why doesn't Kathy come and see me any more?

She (come) and see you if she (have) time.  ☐

h. Lesley's been late for work every morning, this week, you know.

If she (not be) careful, she (lose) her job!  ☐

π—0

2  **Without** listening to the tape, put the verb in brackets in the **correct tense** according to whether the sentence is in the first or second conditional.

Listen and check your answers.

π—0

3  Can you hear the difference between the contractions *I'll* and *I'd*, and *She'll* and *She'd*?

Although the contractions are very short, it is still important to say them. If you have difficulty with this / l / sound, try putting in a short / ʊ / sound between *I* and *'ll*:

I  '  ll
   / ʊ /

or *she* and *'ll* → she'll / ʊ /

**T.9.2.B.** Practise the two contractions by starting with the main verb like this:

■
　help you
/ ʊ /'ll help you
I/ʊ/'ll help you
I/ʊ/'ll help you if you want.

■
　go
/ʊ/'d go
I'd go
I'd go if it was a bit sunnier.

Practise the other sentences in the same way.

4  Read the mini-dialogues with a partner, paying attention to the pronunciation of the contractions.

## ● Intonation

Do this exercise after the Vocabulary and Listening exercises on pages 51–52 of the Student's Book.

### 3 Disagreeing politely

1   **T.9.3.A.** You will hear a couple talking about the sort of home that they are looking for. The woman has lots of ideas about the sort of house that she wants. Sometimes the man agrees with her, but sometimes he is unsure, or disagrees. Listen to his intonation and write **A** if he agrees and **U** if he is unsure.

a.   **W** I think the most important thing is good public transport.

    **A**   **M** Mmm . . .

b.   **W** I really prefer old places to new, modern flats, they've got more atmosphere.

    **U**   **M** Mmm . . .

c.   **W** Mind you, we definitely need somewhere with central heating.

    ☐   **M** Yeah . . .

d.   **W** And I'd really like a nice big kitchen with fitted units.

    ☐   **M** Mmm . . .

e.   **W** If the decorations weren't very good I'd be quite happy to repaint it, wouldn't you?

    ☐   **M** Yeah . . .

f.   **W** And I certainly don't want anyone else's curtains and carpets.

    ☐   **M** No . . .

g.   **W** I'd really like to live in a quiet street . . .

    ☐   **M** Mmm . . .

h.   **W** And it would be lovely if we could get a ground floor flat with a garden.

    ☐   **M** Mmm . . .

i.   **W** Or perhaps just a little patio would be better . . .

    ☐   **M** Mmm . . .

🔑

In all of the sentences the man **seems** to agree, but his intonation shows whether he **really** agrees or not. If he agrees, his intonation starts **high** and **falls** like this:

Mmm . . .

If he is unsure or perhaps disagrees, his intonation starts **high**, **falls** and then goes **up again**:

Mmm . . .

2   Listen again and repeat the man's part. Pay attention to your intonation.

3   **T.9.3.B.** You will hear Jenny and Mark giving their opinions about their ideal place to live.

Listen and answer with *Yes* or *Mmm . . .*, but show by your intonation whether or not you **really** agree with them.

a.     **Jenny**               **You**

If I lived in a city, I'd prefer to live in the centre rather than the suburbs, wouldn't you?

or

🔑

# ● Word focus

## 4 Stress in compound nouns

1 Look at the compound nouns below. They are all possible features of a house. Can you remember what they all mean?

| | |
|---|---|
| bedroom | dining-room |
| French windows | double glazing |
| central heating | utility room |
| fitted wardrobes | living-room |
| air conditioning | fireplace |
| fitted carpets | loft space |

**T.9.4.** Some of the compound nouns have **one** stress, some have **two**. Listen and put them into the correct column.

| 1 ● |
|---|
| bedroom |

| 2 ● ● |
|---|
| French windows |

π—0

2 Some compound nouns are made with **noun** (or **gerund**) + **noun**, some are made with **adjective** + **noun**. Which ones have only **one** stress? Which ones have two?

π—0

Listen again and practise saying the words with the correct stress.

3 Work with a partner and discuss the following questions.

Which of the features in 1 do you think are *essential*, when choosing a home?

Which would be nice to have but not essential, do you think?

Which, if any, would you prefer *not* to have?

## 5 Words ending in *-ture*

1 **T.9.5.** The words below all end in *-ture*. How is this ending pronounced? There is one exception below, can you find it? Listen and repeat.

| | |
|---|---|
| adventure | literature |
| agriculture | mixture |
| architecture | mature |
| culture | nature |
| departure | picture |
| feature | structure |
| furniture | sculpture |
| future | signature |
| lecture | temperature |

Where is the stress in the exception? What about the other words?

π—0

2 Is there any one in your class who is interested in:

agriculture?
architecture?
antique furniture?
modern literature?
ancient literature?
studying nature?
painting pictures?
sculpture?

Ask as many people as you can in five minutes. When you have finished report back to the rest of the class. Who found the most people?

3 Some of the nouns in 1 have adjectives formed with *-tural*. Can you transcribe them?

/ ægrɪ'kʌltʃərəl / _____

/ ɑːkɪ'tektʃərəl / _____

/ 'kʌltʃərəl / _____

/ 'nætʃrəl / _____

/ 'strʌktʃərəl / _____

Use the phonemic spelling to work out the pronunciation and mark the stress, like this ●.

π—0

## ● Everyday English

## 6 Saying mathematical equations

1 Match the words with the signs and then try to complete the gaps below.

×　　add (and) . . .
—　　multiply (by) . . .
＋　　divide (by) . . .
÷　　subtract (from) . . .

a. If you _____ 2 _____ 5, you get 7.

b. If you _____ 3.5 _____ 2, you get 7.

c. If you _____ 6 _____ 13, you get 7.

d. If you _____ 28 _____ 4, you get 7.

T.9.6.A. Listen and check your answers.

π—0

2 Listen again and practise saying the equations.

3 T.9.6.B. Listen and follow the instructions.

a. _____

b. _____

c. _____

d. _____

e. _____

f. _____

What number did you finish with?

Listen again and follow the words in the key.

π—0

4 Work with a partner. Try starting with different numbers between 1 and 10. Do you always end up with the same number? Why is this, do you think?

## 7 Saying weights and measures

1 Below are some terms for saying weights and measures. Match the metric term on the left with the nearest non-metric equivalent on the right.

centimetre　　　ounce
metre　　　　　mile
square metre　　inch
kilometre　　　　pound
litre　　　　　　pint
gram　　　　　　yard
kilogram　　　　acre

T.9.7.A. Listen and check your answers. Repeat the terms paying attention to pronunciation.

π—0

How would the following non-metric measures be expressed in metric terms?

*stone　　gallons　　feet*

π—0

2 T.9.7.B. Listen and complete the conversions.

a. One inch equals _____

b. One foot equals _____

c. One yard equals _____

d. One acre equals _____

e. One mile equals _____

f. One pint equals _____

g. One gallon equals _____

h. One ounce equals _____

i. One pound equals _____

j. One stone equals _____

π—0

3   T.9.7.C.   In Britain, metric measures are now used, but in many situations non-metric measures are still used more often.

Where would you hear the following short conversations? Listen and fill in the first column of the table.

| | Place | Quantity | Goods |
|---|---|---|---|
| a. | greengrocer's or supermarket | a pound | grapes |
| b. | | | |
| c. | | | |
| d. | | | |
| e. | | | |
| f. | | | |
| g. | | | |
| h. | | | |

Listen again and complete the other two columns.

🔑—0

4   Use the words above as prompts to invent short dialogues in British shops, like this:

A  Can I help you?
B  Yes, can I have a *pound of grapes*, please?
A  Certainly, anything else?
B  Yes, two pounds of oranges, please.

# UNIT 10

## ● Sounds

### 1 The sounds / e / and / eɪ /
Ⓔ Ⓕ ⒼⓇ Ⓗ Ⓘ Ⓟ ⓉⓇ

1 Put the verbs in the past tense below into the correct column, according to their vowel sound. One of them might go in either column – which one?

| | | |
|---|---|---|
| dreamt | paid | read |
| waited | lay | laid |
| said | failed | meant |
| made | ate | |

| / e / | / eɪ / |
|---|---|
| *dreamt* | *paid* |
| | |

**T.10.1.** Listen and check your answers. Can you hear the difference between the two sounds clearly?

To make the sound / e / your tongue should be raised at the front of your mouth and your lips should be **open**, like this:

/ e /

To make the sound / eɪ / first make a long / e / sound – / eee / and then raise your tongue slightly and close your lips to make a very short / ɪ / sound, like this:

/ eɪ /

2 Listen again and practise saying the verbs, paying attention to the pronunciation of the vowel.

3 Here are some more verbs in the past tense. Are they pronounced with an / e / or an / eɪ /?

| | | |
|---|---|---|
| f<u>e</u>lt | m<u>e</u>t | l<u>e</u>nt |
| st<u>ay</u>ed | l<u>e</u>ft | h<u>a</u>ted |
| pl<u>ay</u>ed | sl<u>e</u>pt | |

4 Make up sentences with as many of the verbs above in them as possible and then practise saying them correctly.

**Example**
I *waited* while they *ate* their meal, *paid* the bill and *said* goodbye.

52

Do this exercise after the reading on page 56 of the Student's Book.

## 2 The sound / r / and when it is pronounced

**All Nationalities**

1 In British English, *r* is sometimes pronounced and sometimes not. Read and listen to the first paragraph of the article about Ruth Lawrence from page 56 of the Student's Book and notice where *r* is pronounced and where it is not.

> **T.10.2.A.**
> Child p**r**odigy **R**uth Law**r**ence made histo**r**y yesterday when she came a clear first out of the 530 candidates who sat the ent**r**ance exam for St. Hugh's College, Oxford. The all women's college is likely to offer he**r** a scholarship. **R**uth sat th**r**ee three-hour papers – Algebra and Geomet**r**y; Calculus, P**r**obability and Statistics; and Maths, Pu**r**e and Applied. 'I was happy with the first two,' she said yesterday, 'but I wasn't su**r**e about the third.'

2 Now choose the correct rules:

a. *r* is pronounced / is not pronounced when it comes before the vowel sound in the syllable.

b. *r* is pronounced / is not pronounced when it comes after the vowel sound in the syllable.

c. If a word (or syllable) ends in *r*, the *r* is pronounced / is not pronounced if the next word (or syllable) begins with a vowel.

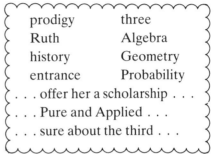

3 **T.10.2.B.** Practise saying these words where *r* is **not** pronounced:

> yesterday    clear
> Oxford       offer
> first        hour
> third        paper
> scholarship

Look at the rest of the text on page 56 and find other words where *r* is silent.

To make the sound / r / turn up the tip of your tongue, like this:

/ r /

The tip of your tongue should **not** touch the roof of your mouth and your tongue should not 'vibrate' – / r / in English is a very **gentle** sound.

4 **T.10.2.C.** Listen and repeat these words and phrases.

> prodigy       three
> Ruth          Algebra
> history       Geometry
> entrance      Probability
> . . . offer her a scholarship . . .
> . . . Pure and Applied . . .
> . . . sure about the third . . .

Listen to the paragraph again and repeat it paying attention to the correct pronunciation of *r*.

5 Here are some more sentences and phrases from the article about Ruth. Use the rules to decide which *r*s are pronounced and which are not. Underline ___ the *r*s that **are** pronounced and cross out (X) the ones that are **not** pronounced. Practise saying the phrases.

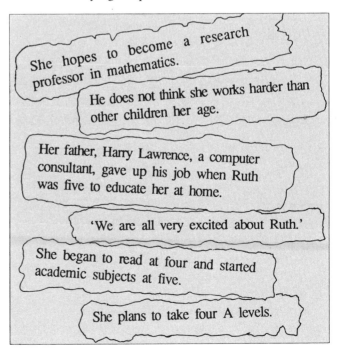

She hopes to become a research professor in mathematics.

He does not think she works harder than other children her age.

Her father, Harry Lawrence, a computer consultant, gave up his job when Ruth was five to educate her at home.

'We are all very excited about Ruth.'

She began to read at four and started academic subjects at five.

She plans to take four A levels.

## ● Connected speech

## 3 Can and can't in connected speech

1 | T.10.3.A. | You will hear a short conversation between three friends. They are talking about typing, word-processing, and computing. Listen and write *can* or *can't* in the gaps.

**Pat** _____ you use a word processor, Julie?

**Julie** No, I'm afraid I'm not very technical. I

_____ type quite fast, but I _____ use a word processor or any kind of computer. How about you?

**Pat** Yes, I _____ use a word processor okay . . .

and really I _____ do everything I want to on

my home computer. I _____ programme it of course!

**Julie** You _____ programme, _____ you Angela? Didn't you do a course when we were at university?

**Angela** Oh yes, I _____ programme all right. My

problem is that I _____ type!

π—0

2 Listen again.

Is *can* stressed or unstressed in the dialogue?
How is it pronounced when it is weak?

Is *can't* stressed or unstressed?
How is it pronounced?

π—0

Notice that if the stress and sounds are said incorrectly, it is often difficult to hear the difference between *can* and *can't* in connected speech.

3 | T.10.3.B. | Practise the phrases with *can* and *can't* from the dialogue. Start with the first stress, like this:

    ☐        ☐
    type quite well
/ kən /
  can type quite well
I can type quite well.

     ☐    ☐     ☐
  can't use a word processor
I can't use a word processor.

Practise the other phrases in the same way.

4 Work in threes. Practise reading the conversation opposite together. Pay attention to your pronunciation of *can* and *can't*.

5 How practical are you? Read the questions below and complete the **first** column, ticking (√) the things that you **can** do, and putting a cross (✗) next to things that you **can't** do.

| | You | Your partner |
|---|---|---|
| Type | | |
| Use a word processor | | |
| Ride a bicycle | | |
| Drive | | |
| Cut hair properly | | |
| Mend a puncture | | |
| Sew on a button | | |
| Make your own clothes | | |
| Swim | | |
| Change a plug | | |
| Put up a shelf | | |
| Cook a family meal | | |

Work with a partner. Tell your partner the things that you *can* and *can't* do, so that your partner can complete the second column in the same way. However, you may say each sentence **only once**, so you must pay attention to your pronunciation.

When you have finished compare your table with your partner's. Did you understand each other correctly? Practise saying again any of the sentences that your partner did not understand.

## 4 Strong and weak forms of at, as, to, for, from, and of – revision

1 **T.10.4.** Listen to these short dialogues at a party and fill in the missing words.

> How long are you here ....... ?

> Only ..... another couple ...days.

> My brother's working ... Macdonald's this summer.

> Oh, what's he working ....?

> ........ a cook!

> Where's the other half ..... that bottle ... whisky?

> You left it .... the bottom .... the stairs.

> Would you like .... come back .... my flat ..... a drink?

> I'd love ....!

π—0

2 Can you remember how the weak forms of these words sound? What about the strong forms?

Listen again and mark the words W if they are weak and S if they are strong.

When are the strong forms used in these dialogues?

π—0

3 Listen and repeat the dialogues, paying attention to the weak and strong forms of these words.

Practise reading the dialogues with a partner.

4 With a partner ask and answer the following questions. Pay attention to your pronunciation of the prepositions.

Where did you go for your holidays last year?
How long did you stay?
Where did you stay?
Have you ever had a holiday job? What did you work as?
What hours did you work? (From ... to ...)
How long did you do it for?

## ● Intonation

Do this exercise after the *Presentation* on page 54 of your Student's Book.

## 5 Question tags with rising and falling intonation

1 **T.10.5.A.** Listen to these dialogues about the news items on page 54 of your Student's Book. Mark the intonation of the question tag ↗ if it goes **up** and ↘ if it goes **down**.

> Have you heard about the robbery of the Holbein painting?

> Yes, but the police managed to catch the thieves, didn't they?

> Have you heard about that man who had all those transplants?

> Yes, isn't it incredible? And he'll be able to go home soon, won't he?

π—0

2 Listen again. In which dialogue do you think that the second speaker is **sure** of what he is saying? In which dialogue do you think he is **really** asking a question because he **isn't** sure?

Complete the rule:

If the intonation of a tag question goes _____ then the speaker is sure of what he is saying. He is only using the question to **check** the information.

If the intonation of the tag question goes _____ then the speaker is not completely sure of what he is saying. He is **really** asking a question.

π—0

3 **T.10.5.B.** Listen and mark the tag questions ↗ or ↘ .

a. You'll be able to come to the party,

   won't you?

b. We can meet again tomorrow,

   can't we?

c. Jan can speak excellent Spanish,

   can't she?

55

d. Your father could play the violin very well, couldn't he?

e. You managed to photocopy that report, didn't you?

f. We'll be able to afford a winter holiday next year, won't we?

g. You could skate really well when you were younger, couldn't you?

h. You managed to pass your driving test first time, didn't you?

4　**T.10.5.C.** Practise the two types of intonation. Remember to stress the **verb** and **not** the pronoun.

The police managed to catch the thieves,

didn't they?

didn't they?

didn't they?

He'll be able to go home soon, won't he?

won't he?

won't he?

Repeat the sentences in 3 with the correct intonation.

Write down five facts about your partner that you think you are sure of, and five facts that you are not really sure of and need to check. Then say things to your partner like this.

**Sure**

You're married, aren't you?

**Not quite sure**

You were in this class last year, weren't you?

## 6 Refusing politely

1　Match up the two halves of these dialogues, like this.

1. Could I borrow this record?

2. Do you mind if I turn off the fire?

3. Could you possibly give me a lift to the station?

4. Do you think I could borrow your jeans?

5. Do you mind if I turn up the music?

6. Could you possibly lend me £5?

7. Would you mind typing this letter for me, before you go home?

8. Do you mind if I smoke?

a. Well, actually . . . we don't like smoking.

b. Well, actually . . . I've only got £5 myself.

c. Well, actually . . . it's not mine.

d. Well, actually . . . there's something wrong with the car.

e. Well, actually . . . they're dirty at the moment.

f. Well, actually . . . I'm in a bit of a hurry.

g. Well, actually . . . I'm a bit cold.

h. Well, actually . . . my flatmate's gone to bed.

**T.10.6.A.** Listen and check your answers.

Notice the intonation in the answer. To make the refusal sound the most polite, the intonation in *actually* should start high, go **down** and then up.

Well, actually . . . it's not mine.

2　**T.10.6.B.** To practise try exaggerating like this:

Well, actually . . . it's not mine.

Well, actually . . . it's not mine.

Well, actually . . . it's not mine.

Listen and repeat the second half of each dialogue, paying attention to intonation.

3   Practise reading the dialogues with a partner and then make up some more of your own, still paying attention to your intonation.

---

Do this exercise after the Vocabulary exercise on page 57 of your Student's Book.

## 7 Intonation with *absolutely*

1   Check the pronunciation of the following words in the dictionary and mark the stress.

| | | |
|---|---|---|
| hilarious | furious | freezing |
| astonishing | vast | filthy |
| fascinating | exhausting | boiling |
| disgusting | delicious | terrifying |

2   Try to guess which of the words above might be used to talk about the following things. Do not write the answers.

a.  The kitchen floor _____

b.  My boss _____

c.  Our neighbour's dog _____

d.  Violence on TV _____

e.  This fish soup _____

f.  The bedroom _____

g.  The inside of the car _____

h.  Her theories about politics _____

i.  The new hypermarket _____

j.  Moving house _____

k.  The new Woody Allen film _____

l.  The end of that book _____

**T.10.7.**   Listen and write in the word which is in fact used.

3   Notice the intonation of *absolutely* + **adjective**. To practise try first exaggerating, like this:

This kitchen floor's absolutely filthy!

This kitchen floor's absolutely filthy!

This kitchen floor's absolutely filthy!

Practise the other adjectives with *absolutely*, using the topics above. Pay attention to your intonation.

4   Look at the tapescript for **T.10.7.A.** on page 104, and practise reading the full dialogues with a partner, still paying attention to pronunciation.

5   Think of *five* situations in your own life recently where you could apply these adjectives. Tell your partner about them.

   **Example**

   My boyfriend cooked a Chinese meal for me last night and it was absolutely delicious!

   *or*

   The hotel where we stayed on our holiday was absolutely filthy!

## ● Word focus

### 8 Saying the names of academic subjects

1  Look at these subjects that you might study at school or university and put them into the correct column below, according to where the stress is.

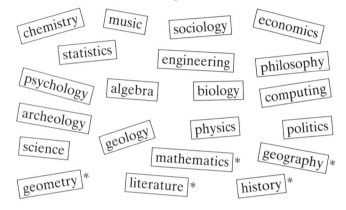

chemistry   music   sociology   economics
statistics   engineering   philosophy
psychology   algebra   biology   computing
archeology   geology   physics   politics
science   mathematics *   geography *
geometry *   literature *   history *

| 1    ● ● | 2    ● ● ● |
|---|---|
| music | chemistry |

| 3    ● ● ● | 4    ● ● ● ● |
|---|---|
| statistics | philosophy |

| 5    ● ● ● ● | 6    ● ● ● ● ● |
|---|---|
| economics | sociology |

*Dictionaries, and native speakers, disagree about how many syllables there are in these words.

🔑

2  T.10.8.A. Listen and check your answers. Practise saying the words correctly.

3  T.10.8.B. You will hear eight students talking about the subject that they study. Listen and write down what the subject is in each case.

a. _____
b. _____
c. _____
d. _____
e. _____
f. _____
g. _____
h. _____

🔑

## ● Everyday English

Do this exercise after the Reading on page 56 of the Student's Book.

### 9 Age and duration as adjectives

Notice the following:

Ruth Lawrence is ten years old. → She's a ten-year-old girl.

The exams she took lasted three hours. → They were three-hour exams.

The course she's going to do at Oxford lasts three years. → It's a three-year course.

Notice too the stress:

She's a ten-year-old girl.

They were three-hour exams.

It's a three-year course.

1  T.10.9. Listen and respond to the information that you hear on the tape, like this:

a. There was a strike where I work that lasted ten months!

*You listen*

What! A ten-month strike!

*You speak*

What! A ten-month strike!

*You listen*

🔑

# UNIT 11

## ● Sounds

### 1 The sounds / b / and / v /

1 **T.11.1.A.** Listen and circle the words you hear.

a. bet          vet
b. best        vest
c. boat        vote
d. bowels    vowels
e. bats        vats

2 Practise making the sounds.

To start the sound / b /, you should press your lips tightly together and push the air in your mouth forward.

You should open your lips and use your voice to make the sound / b /.

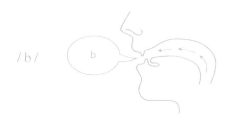

To begin the sound / v /, you should bite your lower lip with your top teeth. You should push out air between your lip and your teeth and use your voice to make the sound.

3 **T.11.1.B.** Listen and repeat the following words.

| / b / | | / v / | |
|-------|-------|-------|------|
| bet    | bats - | vet    | vats |
| best   | ban    | vest   | van  |
| boat   | berry  | vote   | very |
| bowels | bale   | vowels | veil |

Work with a partner and test each other's pronunciation. You say a word and your partner must point to the word that you said.

4 **T.11.1.C.** Practise saying the following sentences, first very slowly, then try saying them very fast.

a. *Vincent brought Brenda a marvellous souvenir vase he'd bought in Venice.*
b. *Bob Viney, the village baker's boy, loves Betty Vole, the barmaid at 'The Bull'.*
c. *Vera Bathory, the Viennese vampire, bathes every evening in buckets of blood.*
d. *A visiting burglar broke Victor Barton's marble bust of Voltaire into various bits.*
e. *Valentine Barlowe, the TV ventriloquist, lives in 'Belleview' – a vast brick villa built in 1812.*

## 2 The sounds / ɔ: / and / əʊ /

(E) (F) (Gr) (H) (I) (J) (P) (Tr)

1 **T.11.2.A.** Listen to the following pairs of words and make sure that you can hear the difference between the vowel sounds.

|  | / ɔ: / | / əʊ / |
|---|---|---|
| a. | cork | coke |
| b. | ball | bowl |
| c. | shore | show |
| d. | noughts | notes |
| e. | saw | sew |

2 **T.11.2.B.** Listen and circle which of the two words you hear in the sentence.

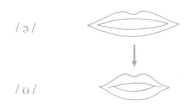

3 Practise making the sounds:

To make the sound / ɔ: /, your lips should be rounded, and your tongue should be raised a little at the **back** of your mouth. / ɔ: / is a long sound.

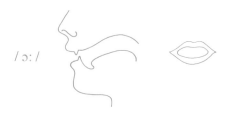

/ əʊ / is a diphthong – a long sound made from putting two vowel sounds together, / ə / + / ʊ /. It starts in the **middle** of your mouth and moves back and up a little. The second sound is very short.

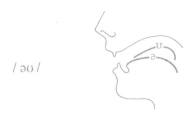

When you make the sound, your lips should look like this:

/ ə /

↓

/ ʊ /

4 Listen to the words in 1 again and repeat them. Make sure that the difference between the two sounds is clear.

5 The vowel sounds in the words below are all marked / əʊ / or / ɔ: /. Work out the pronunciation for each word or phrase.

ɔ:  əʊ
Laura Rhodes

ɔ:  əʊ
Paul Stone

ɔ:  əʊ
Maureen Jones

ɔ:  əʊ
Gordon Hope

ɔ:  əʊ
Audrey Holmes

ɔ:
four

ɔ:
more

ɔ:
all

əʊ
low

əʊ
frozen

əʊ
whole

ɔ:
caught

ɔ:
warm

ɔ:
call

ɔ:
walk

ɔ:
order

əʊ
go

ɔ:
fall

əʊ
over

ɔ:
football

əʊ
home

əʊ
clothes

ɔ:
supporters

əʊ
no

ɔ: əʊ
also

əʊ
totally

əʊ  ɔ:
phonecall

ɔ:
score

əʊ
snow

ɔ:
water

əʊ
though

əʊ
ago

əʊ
below

əʊ
drove

əʊ
local

əʊ
show

**T.11.2.C.** Listen and check your pronunciation.

Work with a partner. Invent your own tongue-twisters using as many of the phrases above as you can.

**Example**

Because of the *snow, Gordon Hope drove all* the *local football supporters home.*

When you have finished, practise saying your sentences and read them out to the class.

60

# ● Connected speech

## 3 Word linking – extra sounds

1  The name *Nicky* from the Reading on page 62 of your Student's Book is short for *Nicola*. Many shortened forms of names are made by adding *-y* or *-ie* to part of the name. What are the following short for?

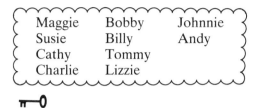

| | | |
|---|---|---|
| Maggie | Bobby | Johnnie |
| Susie | Billy | Andy |
| Cathy | Tommy | |
| Charlie | Lizzie | |

🎵—0

Look what can happen when two of these names are put together with *and* and said quickly:

Billy          and Susie . . .
       └ /j/ ┘

This is because *and* begins with a **vowel** and *Billy* ends with a vowel made at the front of the mouth.

2  **T.11.3.A.** Listen and practise saying the names quickly in pairs.

3  Here are some more names. What sound do they all end with?

| | | |
|---|---|---|
| Linda | Sarah | Sandra |
| Hannah | Sheila | Amanda |
| Laura | Patricia | |

**T.11.3.B.** Listen to them said quickly with *and* between. What extra sound links them together?

🎵—0

Listen again and repeat.

4  Which extra sound might link these names with *and*, if you say them together quickly?

Romeo and Juliet
Othello and Desdemona
Horatio and Hamlet

🎵—0

**T.11.3.C.** Listen and check your answers and then practise saying the pairs of names quickly.

5  Here are some famous names often linked together. Match a name from the left column with one from the right, and then practise saying them together quickly. Which extra sound do you get in each case?

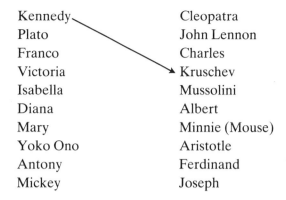

| | |
|---|---|
| Kennedy | Cleopatra |
| Plato | John Lennon |
| Franco | Charles |
| Victoria | Kruschev |
| Isabella | Mussolini |
| Diana | Albert |
| Mary | Minnie (Mouse) |
| Yoko Ono | Aristotle |
| Antony | Ferdinand |
| Mickey | Joseph |

**T.11.3.D.** Listen and check your answers.

🎵—0

6  Now try these tongue-twisters. Which extra sounds can you put in to link them together, when you say them quickly? In what other ways can they be linked together?

a. *My aeroplane arrives in Australia at about eight o'clock in the evening.*
b. *Uncle Alfie and Auntie Elsie always go away at Easter.*
c. *Are you asking us to accept an offer of only eighty pounds?*
d. *Nicky and Laura are off to Italy and Austria again.*
e. *Bruno and Anna are arriving in an hour or so and they're often early.*

**T.11.3.E.** Listen and check your answers. Then practise saying the sentences paying attention to the word linking.

🎵—0

# ● Intonation and sentence stress

## 4 Correcting politely

1 [T.11.4.A.] Listen to these short dialogues. **B** corrects **A**'s mistakes using stress and intonation. Mark the main stress in what **B** says, like this ■.

a. **A** So you've been driving for ten years . . .

   **B** Well, no actually, I've been driving for two years.

b. **A** So you've been studying French for six months . . .

   **B** Well, no actually, I've been studying English for six months.

c. **A** So you've been collecting coins since you left university . . .

   **B** Well, no actually, I've been collecting coins since I left school.

d. **A** So you've been playing the piano since 1980 . . .

   **B** Well, no actually, I've been playing the guitar since 1980.

e. **A** So you've been painting the inside of the house since Monday . . .

   **B** Well, no actually, I've been painting the outside of the house since Monday.

f. **A** So you've been singing in musicals since you were eighteen . . .

   **B** Well, no actually, I've been singing in operas since I was eighteen.

π—O

2 Why are these particular words stressed, do you think?

π—O

Listen again and repeat **B**'s part, paying attention to stress.

3 [T.11.4.B.] Listen and use the prompts below to correct the information on the tape, like this:

a. *Canada*

So you've been living in the United States since you left school . . .

*You listen*

Well, no actually. I've been living in Canada since I left school.

*You speak*

Well, no actually. I've been living in Canada since I left school.

*You listen*

b. *a few months*
c. *for four hours*
d. *learning*
e. *tennis*
f. *writing*
g. *meat*
h. *cycling*
i. *1971*
j. *ironing*

Pay attention to stress.

π—O

## 5 Showing surprise in *Wh*- questions

1 Try to complete **B**'s part in the dialogues below:

a. **A** I've been learning to drive for seventeen years, you know.

   **B** How _____ did you say?

b. **A** They've got sixteen children, you know.

   **B** How _____ did you say?

c. **A** She washes her hair at least six times a week, you know.

   **B** How _____ did you say?

d. **A** She's 120 years old, you know.

   **B** How _____ did you say?

e.  **A** He's 6′8″ tall you know.

   **B** How _____ did you say?

f.  **A** The nearest house is 20 miles away, you know.

   **B** How _____ did you say?

g.  **A** The outer walls of this house are three feet thick, you know.

   **B** How _____ did you say?

h.  **A** I bought it in the sale for £10, you know.

   **B** How _____ did you say?

**T.11.5.A.** Listen and check your answers.

Notice the intonation pattern in these *Wh-* questions. Normally the intonation goes **down** at the end of *Wh-* questions:

How long have you been learning to drive for?

But because the speaker here is using the question to show *surprise* the intonation goes *up* at the end of the question, like this:

How long did you say?

2  **T.11.5.B.** To practise, try first humming the surprised intonation like this:

MM MM mm mm MM? ......
How long did you say?

MM MM-mm mm mm MM? ......
How many did you say?

MM MM-mm mm mm MM? ......
How often did you say?

3  Listen to the dialogues in 1 again and repeat **B**'s part paying attention to your intonation.

Notice that this type of intonation can be used with all sorts of *Wh-* questions, not just questions with *How.*

4  **T.11.5.C.** You will hear a student talking about a colleague of his, who is very eccentric. Listen and respond with surprise, using the question words below as prompts, like this.

a.  *Where?*

One of my colleagues lives in a caravan in the middle of the country.

*You listen*

*You speak*

Where does he live?

Where does he live?

*You listen*

b.  *Who?*
c.  *How many?*
d.  *How far?*
e.  *How?*
f.  *What?*
g.  *What?*
h.  *What?*

Pay attention to your intonation.

● **Word focus**

**6** Adjectives ending in *-able*

1  Look at the clues in brackets and fill in the adjectives.

a.  (a business which makes a profit)

   a _____ business

b.  (a car you can't rely on)

   an _____ car

c.  (a mistake you can understand)

   an _____ mistake.

d.  (a book that's good to read)

   a _____ book

e. (a chap you can depend on)

a _____ chap

f. (an evening you can't forget)

an _____ evening

g. (behaviour you can't accept)

_____ behaviour

h. (a story you can't believe)

an _____ story

i. (a situation you can't avoid)

an _____ situation

j. (a rule you can't break)

an _____ rule

k. (a person you like)

a _____ person

l. (a madman you can't control)

an _____ madman

2 **T.11.6.A.** Listen and check your answers. Try to work out where the stress is in each word and then listen again to check.

Practise saying the adjectives putting the stress on the correct syllable.

🔑

3 Adverbs ending in *-ably*

Adjectives ending in *-able* can make adverbs ending in *-ably*. There is no change in stress and the number of syllables remains the same:

**adjective** profitable **adverb** profitably

Fill in the adverbs. Use the words in brackets to help you. Sometimes you need to add the prefix *un-*.

a. He was _____ very tired at the end of a long week. (*understand*)

b. We spent the weekend most

_____ – sunbathing and swimming in the lake. (*enjoy*)

c. His ex-wife behaved _____ – making him wash in cold water every morning. (*reason*)

d. The business ran _____ for five years and he lost all his money. (*profit*)

e. Who's that _____ good-looking young man in the corner? (*believe*)

f. She looked after the children very

_____ while their parents were out, and there were no problems. (*capable*)

g. The quality of these photographs is

_____ bad – let's send them back! (*accept*)

h. That man was _____ rude to me – I shall never speak to him again. (*forgive*)

**T.11.6.B.** Listen and check your answers.

🔑

4 Practise saying the adverbs paying attention to stress.

## 7 Stress in compound nouns

1 Put one word in each space to make four compound nouns each time.

a. paint
tooth
clothes _____
hair

b. birthday
Christmas
Valentine _____
get well

c. washing
coffee
sewing _____
answering

d. black
notice
chess _____
score

e. cheque
recipe
address _____
telephone

f. wrapping
writing
note _____
wall

g. drinks
filing
medicine _____
china

h. table
desk
wall _____
reading

i. climbing
football
wellington _____
riding

j. rolling
drawing
hair _____
safety

k. flower
coffee
pepper _____
tea

l. book
suit
pencil _____
brief

🔑

(The key shows if the compounds are written as one word or two words.)

Which word carries the main stress in each case?

🔑

2   **T.11.7.**   Listen and practise saying the compound nouns, paying attention to stress.

## ● Everyday English

---

## 8 Saying abbreviations

Some abbreviations are pronounced as words:

**Example** AIDS (Acquired Immune Deficiency Syndrome) = / eɪdz /

Others are spelt out letter by letter:

**Example** BBC (British Broadcasting Corporation) = / bi: bi: si:/

1   **T.11.8.A.**   Listen to the following list of abbreviations and circle **only the ones that can be pronounced as words.**

| | |
|---|---|
| AA | Automobile Association |
| AD | *Anno Domini*; the year of our Lord |
| AM | *Ante Meridiem*; before noon |
| BC | Before Christ |
| CND | Campaign for Nuclear Disarmament |
| DIY | Do it yourself |
| EEC | European Economic Community |
| IRA | Irish Republican Army |
| NASA | National Aeronautics and Space Administration |
| NATO | North Atlantic Treaty Organization |
| OAP | Old age pensioner |
| OPEC | Organization of Petroleum-Exporting Countries |
| RAF | Royal Air Force |
| UFO | Unidentified Flying Object |
| USA | United States of America |
| USSR | Union of Soviet Socialist Republics |
| VAT | Value Added Tax |
| VIP | Very Important Person |

2   Practise saying the abbreviations correctly.

3   Can you guess which of the abbreviations above is used in these?

a. He used to be a pilot in the _____ .

b. Sean O'Reilly, a former member of the _____ died in prison yesterday.

c. The Queen was given a _____ welcome by the Canadian Prime Minister this morning.

d. _____ protesters tried to stop the Prime Minister opening a new nuclear missile base in Britain this afternoon.

e. The government will introduce higher _____ rates on cigarettes and alcohol from next year.

f. _____ has put up the price of crude oil by 5% this month.

g. A Swiss doctor has discovered an effective, low-cost cure for _____ .

h. Make your own loft room, greenhouse or conservatory! _____ magazine tells you how.

i. Socrates died in 399 _____ .

j. _____ ministers will meet later today in Brussels to discuss the growing international problem of unemployment.

**T.11.8.B.**   Listen and check your answers.

# UNIT 12

## ● Sounds

### 1 The sound / ŋ /
(E) (F) (J) (P)

In English, the sound / ŋ / always comes in the middle or at the end of a syllable – never at the beginning:

sing / sɪŋ /   think / θɪŋk /

1   **T.12.1.A.** Listen to these pairs of words and if the word with a / ŋ / sound comes first, write 1 and if the word with a / ŋ / sound comes second write 2 .

a. _____   d. _____

b. _____   e. _____

c. _____   f. _____

🔑—0

To make the sound / ŋ / the air should come out through your nose as in the sound / n /. But your tongue should touch the back of your mouth, **not** the front:

/ n /

/ ŋ /

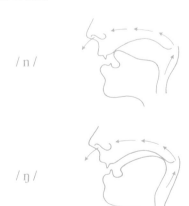

2   Listen again and repeat the words, making sure that the difference between the sounds / ŋ / and / n / is clear.

3   If there is another syllable after *ng* then sometimes the *g* is pronounced and sometimes it is not. Look at the words below and decide whether or not the *g* is pronounced.

finger      tango
longer      ringing
mango       banging
single      hunger
Hungary     strongest
singer      coathanger

**T.12.1.B.** Listen and check your answers.

🔑—0

### 2 The sound / aʊ /
(All Nationalities)

1   **T.12.2.A.** In English many words spelt with *ou* or *ow* are pronounced / aʊ /. Listen to these groups of words and circle the one which is *not* pronounced / aʊ /.

a. hour     sour     four     flour
b. tower    power    shower   lower
c. show     now      cow      how
d. shout    about    route    sprout
e. town     grown    brown    down

🔑—0

66

To practise making the sound / aʊ / you should first practise the sound / æ /. Your mouth should be **open** and you should make the sound at the front of your mouth with your tongue down like this:

/ æ /

To make / aʊ / add a short / ʊ / after the long / æ / sound.

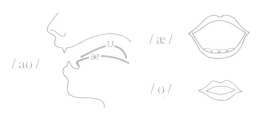

/ aʊ /

/ æ /

/ ʊ /

2   Listen again and practise saying the words with / aʊ / correctly.

3   Look at the sentences below and discuss with a partner what order they should go in. (There may be more than one possible answer.)

a.  / lying / this morning / £50 / I found / in town / on the ground / I was / when.
b.  / 's going to / now / round / Laura / you / the house / show /.
c.  / downstairs / shower room / in the / we caught / mouse / little brown / a / this morning.
d.  / and / they've got / you know / town / country / house / house / a / a /.
e.  / from the / they / to the / tower / ground / cow / of the / lowered / the / window / .

4   T.12.2.B.   Listen and compare your answers with the tape.

Practise saying the sentences pronouncing the / aʊ / sounds correctly.

● **Connected speech**

**3** Understanding fast speech

1   T.12.3.   Listen and write the number of words you hear in the box on the left. (*I'm* = two words)

a. [ ]  _____ doing
        _____ Thursday night?

b. [ ]  _____ party
        _____ weekend, _____ ?

c. [ ]  _____ going _____ tonight,
        _____ staying _____ ?

d. [ ]  _____ , _____ manager
        _____ until _____ lunch.

e. [ ]  _____ Dave
        _____ tomorrow _____ ?

f. [ ]  _____ front
        _____ theatre _____ night
        _____ seven.

Listen again and fill in the missing words.

2   Which words do you think are **stressed** in each sentence? Which words do you think are **weak**? How do you think the weak words are pronounced?

Listen again and check to see if you were correct.

Practise reading the sentences paying attention to the stress and weak forms.

## 4 Word linking in informal speech – revision

1   **T.12.4.**   If you listen to the dialogue at the beginning of Unit 12 in the Student's Book it is a rather **formal** conversation. But listen to a similar dialogue which is very *informal*:

**Steve**   Hello this is Steve – ca**n** I spea**k** to Aliso**n** please?

**Paul**   I'**m** afraid she's havi**ng** a showe**r** at the moment – can she ring you back?

**Steve**   Mmm . . . well, a**ll** righ**t**, but I'**m** goi**ng** out i**n** a couple of minutes. I'**ll** be bac**k** i**n** about two hours okay – can she phone me bac**k** then?

**Paul**   I thin**k** she's goi**ng** out later herself – oh ha**ng** on, she's just comi**ng** out of the shower – I'**ll** pass yo**u** over t**o** he**r** okay . . .

Could you catch all the words? If not listen again until you can.

2   Look at the letters in heavy print at the beginnings and ends of words, and try to answer the following questions:

    a. Which sounds **link onto** the next word?
    b. Which sounds **disappear**?
    c. Which sounds **change** so that the words link together more easily?
    d. Which sounds have an **extra sound** between them to help them to link together?

Listen to the dialogue in short sections and practise the different types of linking yourself.

3   Practise reading the dialogue with a partner at the same speed that it is on the tape.

## ● Intonation

Do this exercise after the sentence combination exercise on page 71 of the Student's Book.

## 5 Intonation in sentences with several clauses

1   Look at the sentence about Bert Langley on page 71 of the Student's Book and then try to re-write the following information in the same way.

    a. Linda McCartney is the wife of Paul McCartney. She lives a quiet life in the country.

    b. Mary Padley is a woman.
       She is 103 years old.
       She lives in London.
       She smokes 60 cigarettes a day.

    c. Linda Smaje is a housewife.
       She is 39 years old.
       She comes from London.
       She has gone bankrupt because of credit card spending.

    d. Olive Gibbs is a woman.
       She is 72 years old.
       She comes from Sussex.
       She has travelled the world in a camping van.

    e. Nicky Bennett-Rees is a nurse.
       She lives in London.
       She is taking part in a sponsored climb of Mt. Kilimanjaro.

    f. Ruth Lawrence is a girl.
       She is ten years old.
       She comes from Huddersfield.
       She has won a scholarship to Oxford.

2   **T.12.5.A.**   Listen and compare your answers.

Notice the intonation. In **all** parts of the sentence the intonation normally goes **down**, but the extra information (given between commas) normally has **lower** intonation than the rest of the sentence:

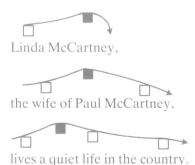

It is also important to pause at the commas.

**T.12.5.B.** Practise by first humming the intonation, like this:

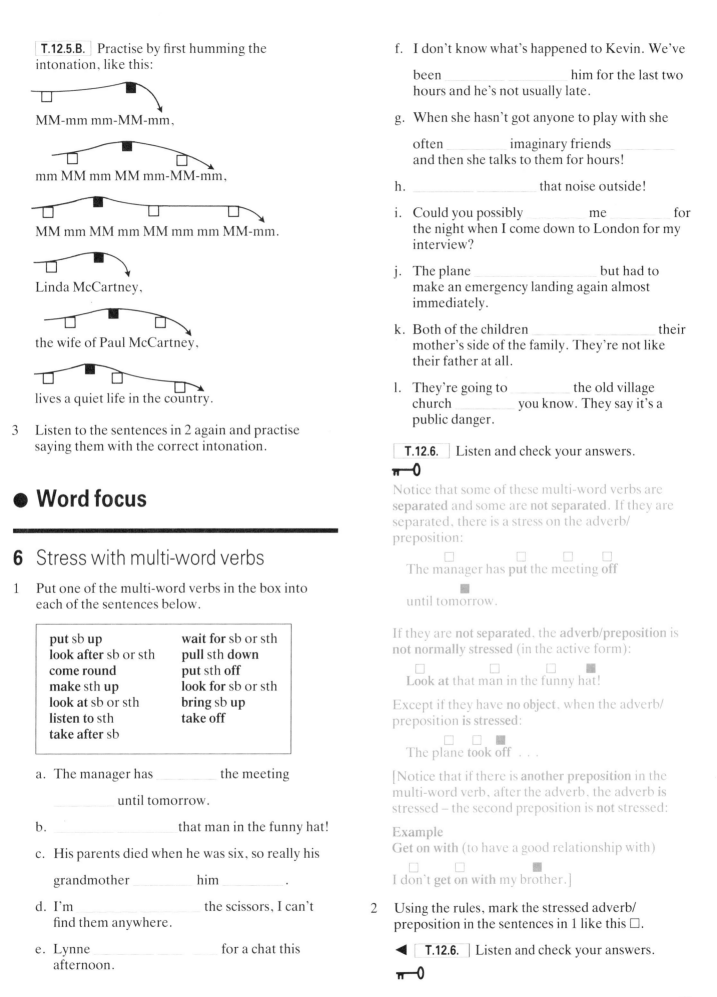

MM-mm mm-MM-mm,

mm MM mm MM mm-MM-mm,

MM mm MM mm MM mm mm MM-mm.

Linda McCartney,

the wife of Paul McCartney,

lives a quiet life in the country.

3  Listen to the sentences in 2 again and practise saying them with the correct intonation.

# ● Word focus

## 6  Stress with multi-word verbs

1  Put one of the multi-word verbs in the box into each of the sentences below.

| | |
|---|---|
| **put** sb **up** | **wait for** sb or sth |
| **look after** sb or sth | **pull** sth **down** |
| **come round** | **put** sth **off** |
| **make** sth **up** | **look for** sb or sth |
| **look at** sb or sth | **bring** sb **up** |
| **listen to** sth | **take off** |
| **take after** sb | |

a.  The manager has _____ the meeting _____ until tomorrow.

b.  _____ that man in the funny hat!

c.  His parents died when he was six, so really his grandmother _____ him _____ .

d.  I'm _____ the scissors, I can't find them anywhere.

e.  Lynne _____ for a chat this afternoon.

f.  I don't know what's happened to Kevin. We've been _____ _____ him for the last two hours and he's not usually late.

g.  When she hasn't got anyone to play with she often _____ imaginary friends _____ and then she talks to them for hours!

h.  _____ _____ that noise outside!

i.  Could you possibly _____ me _____ for the night when I come down to London for my interview?

j.  The plane _____ _____ but had to make an emergency landing again almost immediately.

k.  Both of the children _____ _____ their mother's side of the family. They're not like their father at all.

l.  They're going to _____ the old village church _____ you know. They say it's a public danger.

**T.12.6.**  Listen and check your answers.

Notice that some of these multi-word verbs are **separated** and some are **not separated**. If they are separated, there is a stress on the adverb/preposition:

The manager has **put** the meeting **off** until tomorrow.

If they are **not separated**, the **adverb/preposition** is **not normally stressed** (in the active form):

**Look at** that man in the funny hat!

Except if they have **no object**, when the adverb/preposition **is stressed**:

The plane **took off** . . .

[Notice that if there is **another preposition** in the multi-word verb, after the adverb, the adverb is stressed – the second preposition is **not** stressed:

**Example**
**Get on with** (to have a good relationship with)

I don't **get on with** my brother.]

2  Using the rules, mark the stressed adverb/preposition in the sentences in 1 like this □.

◀  **T.12.6.**  Listen and check your answers.

## ● **Everyday English**

Do this exercise after the reading on pages 67–8 of the Student's Book.

## 7 Scientific and mathematical vocabulary

1 Look at the scientific and mathematical words below. Are they the same in your language? Use a dictionary to check the pronunciation in English, and the meaning of any that you don't understand.

Remember to mark the stress.

●

| | |
|---|---|
| oxygen | diameter |
| solar energy | hydro-electric power |
| astronaut | nitrogen |
| globe | rotation |
| nuclear power | circumference |
| axis | planet |
| hydrogen | space |
| radius | |

π━0

2 Work in pairs. Sort the words out into five groups of three words associated with each other. The first word in each group has been given:

| a | b |
|---|---|
| oxygen | diameter |

| c | d |
|---|---|
| solar energy | astronaut |

| e |
|---|
| globe |

**T.12.7.** Listen and check your answers.

π━0

Can you think of any other words that could go in each group? Use your dictionary to check the correct pronunciation in English.

70

## 8 Saying the names of geographical features

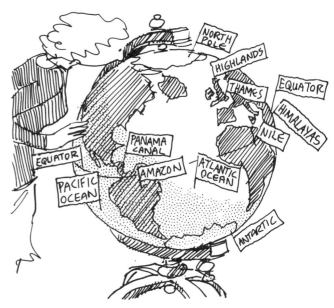

1 Look at the famous geographical features below – are there any that you do not recognize? If so, find out what they are in your language.

Try to guess how they are pronounced in English.

| | |
|---|---|
| the Amazon | the Thames |
| the Panama Canal | the Nile |
| the Antarctic | the Highlands |
| the Rhine | the Suez Canal |
| the Danube | the Arctic Circle |
| the South Pole | the Pacific Ocean |
| the Equator | the Atlantic Ocean |
| the Himalayas | the North Pole |
| the Tropics | the Andes |
| the Mediterranean | the Sahara Desert |
| the Pyrenees | |

2 **T.12.8.A.** Listen and count how many you guessed correctly. Practise saying the ones you guessed incorrectly.

3 **T.12.8.B.** Now listen and answer the questions on the tape like this. (All the answers are in the box above.)

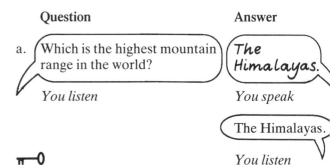

| Question | Answer |
|---|---|
| a. Which is the highest mountain range in the world? | The Himalayas. |
| *You listen* | *You speak* |
| | The Himalayas. |
| | *You listen* |

π━0

# UNIT 13

## ● Sounds

### 1 The sounds / ʊ / and / u: /

**T.13.1.A.** Listen to the following phrases and underline the sound / ʊ / like this _____ and the sound / u: / like this ⌇⌇⌇⌇ . Listen to the example a few times to make sure that you can hear the difference between the two sounds.

**Example**

Good food    The School Rules

push or pull?

Cookery Book    News Bulletin

A New Look    Football Pools

A book of cartoons

Good Afternoon    A room with a view

To make the sound / u: / your tongue should go up at the back of your mouth and your lips should look like this:

/ u: /

To make the sound / ʊ / your tongue should be **lower** in your mouth and your lips should look like this:

/ ʊ /

/ u: / is a **long** sound – / ʊ / is a **short** sound.

2 Listen again and repeat the phrases, paying attention to your pronunciation of the two sounds.

Notice that some words beginning with the letter *u* begin with the sound / j / ( + / u: / ).

University / ˌjuːnɪˈvɜːsɪtɪ /

usually / ˈjuːʒəlɪ /

This happens sometimes even if there's a consonant sound before the / u: / sound:

future / ˈfjuːtʃə /

news / njuːz / *US* / nuːz /

Tuesday / ˈtjuːzdɪ / *US* / ˈtuː- /

3 Look at the / u: / sounds underlined in the words below and say which ones have an extra / j / sound in front of them.

| | | |
|---|---|---|
| beauty | stupid | tune |
| few | cucumber | useful |
| do | fool | cute |
| excuse | produce | fume |
| boots | united | tool |
| flew | cool | view |
| Duke | fuel | |

**T.13.1.B.** Listen and check your answers.
**NB** *US* pronunciation of the following is different:

Duke / du:k /
stupid / ˈstu:pɪd /
produce / -ˈdu:s /
tune / tu:n /

🔑—0

4 Below are some common English sayings and proverbs. The meaning of some is quite clear, but can you work out what the others mean?

a. No news is good news.
b. I wouldn't like to be in your shoes.
c. He's getting too big for his boots.
d. The proof of the pudding is in the eating.
e. It's too good to be true.
f. He's got a screw loose.

**T.13.1.C.** Look at the sayings again and try to decide where the / u: / sounds are, and where the / ʊ / sounds are. Listen and check your answers.

🔑—0

Listen again and practise saying the sentences paying attention to the two sounds.

## ● Connected speech

### 2 Weak forms with passives

1 **T.13.2.A.** Listen to the sentences only **once**, and without stopping the tape. Write P if the sentence is in the **passive** and A if the sentence is in the **active**.

| | | |
|---|---|---|
| a. *P* | d. _____ | g. _____ |
| b. _____ | e. _____ | h. _____ |
| c. _____ | f. _____ | i. _____ |

🔑—0

Notice that when there are several auxiliary verbs only the **main verb** is normally stressed:

☐ ☐ ☐ ☐
A hundred and seventy-three people **have been**
■
**killed**.

☐ ☐ ■
Six men **are being questioned** . . .

☐ ☐ ■
The Prince and Princess of Wales **have been**
■ ☐ ☐
**enjoying** a day of sightseeing . . .

The auxiliary verbs then normally become *weak*:

/ həv bɪn / ■
. . . have been killed . . .

/ ə / ■
. . . are being questioned . . .

/ həv bɪn / ■
. . . have been enjoying . . .

2 ◄ **T.13.2.A.** Listen to the sentences again and practise saying them, paying attention to stress and weak forms.

3 **T.13.2.B.** Use the words below as prompts to make up your own news items about the pictures. Decide which **tense** you should use, and whether it should be **passive** or **active**. Respond like this:

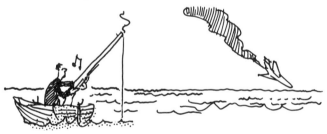

a. **American warplane / shoot down over / Mediterranean**

An American warplane has been shot down over the Mediterranean.

*You speak*

An American warplane has been shot down over the Mediterranean.

*You listen*

Pay attention to stress and weak forms.

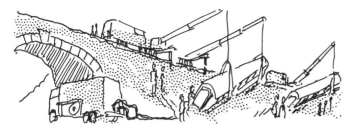

b. **43 people / kill / train crash near Glasgow**

c. **12 British soccer fans / arrest / Paris / last night for hooliganism**

d. **British company, General Engines / sell / next month / to / American electrical company**

e. **there / be / general elections / New Zealand today**

f. **man / question / tonight / London police / about / murder of / 7-year old girl**

g. **the Queen / visit / isolated Amazonian tribe today during / official visit to Brazil**

h. **oldest man in Britain / die / Birmingham hospital / today / age 113**

Do this exercise after the Vocabulary exercise on Opposites on page 75 of the Student's Book.

## 3 Word linking – extra / j / and / w / sounds

1   The words *very* and *too* are often confused in English. Do you have two different words in your language, or just one? If you have only one, do you know the difference between the two words in English?

2   Complete these pairs of dialogues with *very* or *too*. Use each word only once for each pair.

a.  i.  Excuse me for asking, but how much did the train ticket to Newcastle cost?

It was _____ expensive, about £60.

ii. Why didn't you come here on the train?

It was _____ expensive, about £60.

b. i. It seems quite safe in this area at night . . .

Actually, it's _____ unsafe.

ii. Why didn't you travel up here in that old car of yours?

Actually, it's _____ unsafe.

c. i. How did you feel about things when you woke up this morning?

To be honest, I was still _____ annoyed.

ii. Why didn't you come out for a drink with the boss last night?

To be honest, I was still _____ annoyed.

d. i. Why didn't Mary apply for that job, do you know?

I'm not sure, but I think she was _____ old . . .

ii. How old was her grandmother when she died?

I'm not sure, but I think she was _____ old . . .

**T.13.3.A.** Listen and check your answers.

Look at **B**'s responses again. Notice that when *very* + **adjective** is said **quickly**, there is often an extra / j / sound between the two words to link them together.

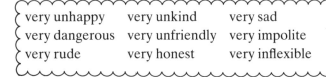
very     expensive

Why is this? What kind of sound do all the adjectives in **B**'s part begin with?

3 **T.13.3.B.** Practise saying these expressions, putting in the extra / j / sound to link the words together **where possible**.

| | | |
|---|---|---|
| very unhappy | very unkind | very sad |
| very dangerous | very unfriendly | very impolite |
| very rude | very honest | very inflexible |

Look at **B**'s responses in the dialogues above again. This time notice that when *too* + **adjective** is said quickly, there is often an extra / w / sound between the two words to link them together.

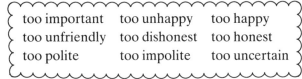
too     expensive

Again notice that this can only happen with words that begin with a vowel sound.

4 **T.13.3.C.** Practise saying these expressions, putting in the extra / w / sound to link the two words together, **where possible**.

| | | |
|---|---|---|
| too important | too unhappy | too happy |
| too unfriendly | too dishonest | too honest |
| too polite | too impolite | too uncertain |

5 Listen to the dialogues in 2 again and repeat **B**'s part, paying attention to the extra linking sounds.

Practise reading the dialogues with a partner.

6 With your partner, invent four two-line dialogues similar to those in 2. Use some of the expressions in 3 and 4 above in your dialogues. Read your dialogues out to the rest of the class, at a **fast** conversational speed. Pay attention to the extra linking sounds.

# ● Intonation and sentence stress

## 4 Intonation with *quite* – showing reservation

*Quite* can have two different meanings according to where the main stress (and intonation) is.

Type A: It's quite interesting   (= yes, it's definitely interesting)

Type B: It's quite interesting   (= but **not very** interesting)

1   T.13.4.A.   Listen to the dialogues and mark them   *A*   if they are the first type and   *B*   if they are the second type.

a. What did Mike say about the argument?

A — Oh, he was quite honest about it.

b. Didn't you think the play was amusing?

It was quite funny.

c. Steve's a really nice person, isn't he?

Mmm . . . he's quite selfish, you know.

d. What are the people like at your new job?

They're quite nice.

e. How was the film last night?

I thought it was quite disappointing.

f. I really enjoyed the final of the tennis match, didn't you?

It was quite good.

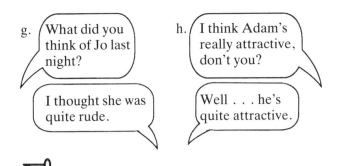

g. What did you think of Jo last night?

I thought she was quite rude.

h. I think Adam's really attractive, don't you?

Well . . . he's quite attractive.

2   T.13.4.B.   Practise the intonation. Try humming it first like this:

Type A:  . . . mm MM MM-mm-mm ......
         It's quite interesting . . .

Type B:  . . . mm MM MM-mm-mm ......
         It's quite interesting . . .

Listen and repeat the second part of each dialogue in 1, paying attention to your intonation.

3   Practise reading the dialogues with a partner.

4   Two friends have spent the summer camping in France. Now they are telling some other friends about it.

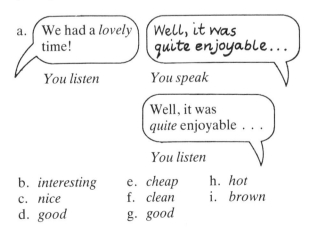

T.13.4.C.   **A** is very enthusiastic, but **B** has some reservations. Listen and take **B**'s part, using the prompt words below, like this:

a. We had a *lovely* time!

*You listen*

Well, it was quite enjoyable...

*You speak*

Well, it was *quite* enjoyable . . .

*You listen*

b. *interesting*    e. *cheap*    h. *hot*
c. *nice*           f. *clean*    i. *brown*
d. *good*           g. *good*

Pay attention to stress and intonation.

# ● Word focus

Do this exercise after the Reading on page 74 of your Student's Book.

## 5 Adjectives ending in -al

1 In the reading on page 74 of the Student's Book there are **eight** adjectives ending in -al. Can you find them?

 T.13.5.A. Listen and check your answers.

 How is the -al at the end of the adjectives pronounced?

 What about -cial?

 Listen again and repeat the words, paying attention to the pronunciation of the endings.

2 What is the -al adjective from the following words?

> finance      practice
> society      politics
> nation       sex
> commerce     theory
> nature

 T.13.5.B. Listen and check your answers.

 Practise saying the words, still paying attention to the pronunciation of the endings.

3 T.13.5.C. Like other adjectives, adjectives ending in -al form adverbs with -ly. Listen to the sentences and write down the adverb that you hear in them.

 a. _____
 b. _____
 c. _____
 d. _____
 e. _____
 f. _____
 g. _____
 h. _____

 How is the ending -ally pronounced in these sentences?

Practise saying the adverbs, pronouncing the ending correctly.

4 Look at the adjectives you formed again and practise saying the adverb in each case.

5 Use the words in brackets to help you to complete the following sentences. Decide whether to use an adjective (ending in -al) or an adverb (ending in -ally). You may have to add to prefixes to form **opposites**, like un-, im- etc.

 a. _____, I agree with you. (*person*)

 b. Some people are against vegetarianism because they think it's (*nature*) _____

 c. What you are asking is _____ impossible. (*physics*)

 d. He's very intelligent, but unfortunately, he's rather _____. (*practice*)

 e. The area of Eastern England called New Holland has that name because it's

 _____ very similar to Holland. (*geography*)

 f. I'll tell you this _____, but please don't tell anyone that I told you – if you do, I'll be in serious trouble. (*office*)

 g. This is a _____ disaster. (*nation*)

 h. Many people believe that there will be serious

 _____ problems in the next century. (*ecology*)

 i. There are important _____ differences between the various parts of Spain. (*region*)

 j. He smokes an _____ cigar. (*occasion*)

 T.13.5.D. Listen and check your answers.

## ● Everyday English

## 6 Saying the names of cities

1 Look at the cities below – do you know which country they are all in? Do they have the same names in your language, or not? Mark the ones with the **same** names with a tick (√), and the ones with different names with a star ∗.

| | | |
|---|---|---|
| London | Venice | Lisbon |
| Prague | Cairo | Paris |
| Vienna | Warsaw | The Hague |
| Cambridge | Moscow | Brussels |
| Birmingham | Oxford | Tokyo |
| Athens | Chicago | Sidney |
| Rome | Munich | |

2 **T.13.6.** How do you think the names are pronounced in English? Listen and check to see how many you guessed correctly. Practise saying the ones that you guessed wrongly.

3 Can you remember which cities the other students in your class have visited? If not make guesses. Write sentences like this:

**Example** *I think Anna's been to Paris.*
*Maybe Maria's been to London.*

Ask questions to check what you have written, like this:

> You've been to Paris, haven't you, Anna?

> Have you been to London, Maria?

Pay attention to your pronunciation of the names of the cities.

Who wrote the most correct sentences?

## 7 Saying temperatures

1 **T.13.7.** A couple are thinking about where to go for their holidays. Listen to the dialogue and fill in the missing words.

M _____ was the

_____ in Lisbon yesterday?

W It was 86 _____

_____ .

M _____ in

centigrade?

W It's . . . 30 _____

_____ .

⚷—0

Notice that *two* different ways of saying the temperature are commonly used in Britain – we talk about either *degrees centigrade* or *degrees fahrenheit*.

2 Practise reading the dialogue with a partner.

3 Work with a partner again. One of you is **A**, one of you is **B**. It is January and both of you want a winter holiday. **A** wants some *winter sun* and does not care how far he or she travels. **B** wants to visit a European city and would like to be somewhere where there is a good chance of *snow*.

**A** should look at the newspaper weather report on **this** page and **B** should look at the one on the **next** page. Have dialogues like the one in 1. Ask and answer in turn. Fill in the missing temperatures.

**A**

| | °F | °C |
|---|---|---|
| ATHENS | ___ | ___ |
| CAIRO | ___ | ___ |
| LONDON | 43 | 6 |
| MOSCOW | 30 | −1 |
| NAIROBI | ___ | ___ |
| PARIS | 50 | 10 |
| ROME | 57 | 14 |
| SYDNEY | ___ | ___ |
| TEL AVIV | ___ | ___ |
| TOKYO | ___ | ___ |
| VIENNA | 41 | 5 |
| WARSAW | 25 | −4 |

**B**

|  | °F | °C |
|---|---|---|
| ATHENS | 57 | 14 |
| CAIRO | 66 | 19 |
| LONDON | —— | —— |
| MOSCOW | —— | —— |
| NAIROBI | 77 | 25 |
| PARIS | —— | —— |
| ROME | —— | —— |
| SYDNEY | 73 | 23 |
| TEL AVIV | 65 | 18 |
| TOKYO | 46 | 8 |
| VIENNA | —— | —— |
| WARSAW | —— | —— |

Which do you think would be the most suitable places for the sort of holiday you want?

---

## 8 Saying abbreviations in names and addresses

1 Look at the letter on page 72 of the Student's Book. You will notice that when we write names and addresses, we often use abbreviations. What do the abbreviations below mean? How do we say them?

| | | | |
|---|---|---|---|
| Mr | Mrs | Ms | Dr |
| Prof | Co | & Co | Ltd |
| Ave | Rd | St | Sq |
| N | S | E | W |
| Nth | Sth | SE | SW |
| NE | NW | c/o | |
| St. (for example *St. Mark's*) | | | |

T.13.8.A. Listen and check your pronunciation.

π—0

2 How would you say the following names and addresses?

Dr James Harvey,
15 Pelham Ave,
Sth Leaming.

Goodhand & Co Ltd,
73 Ferriby St,
St. Albans.

Ms Louise Hammond,
c/o Northern Trading Co,
3 Town Hall Sq,
Eastford.

Prof Helen Leach,
97 Springfield Rd,
London SE 21.

Mr and Mrs G Shaw
16 Waterford Sq,
London W 1.

T.13.8.B. Listen and check your answers.

π—0

# UNIT 14

● **Sounds**

## 1 The sounds / j / and / dʒ /
Ⓓ Ⓔ Ⓕ Ⓖⓡ Ⓟ Ⓣⓡ

1   **T.14.1.A.**   Do you know what the words below mean? Listen and write them in the spaces below in the order that you hear them on the tape.

| Yale | yet | jet |
| your | jaw | use |
| jail | yolk | juice |
| joke | | |

a. _____   _____

b. _____   _____

c. _____   _____

d. _____   _____

e. _____   _____

π—0

Can you hear the difference between the sounds / j / and / dʒ /? If not, listen to the pairs of words again.

To make the sound / j / your tongue **doesn't** touch the roof of your mouth.

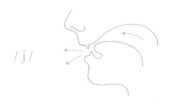
/ j /

If you have problems with the sound / j / you can try starting with / i: / like this:

iii: → yes
 ii: → yes
  i: → yes

/ dʒ / is a combination of / d / and / ʒ /.

/ d /

To start the sound / dʒ / the front of your tongue should touch the roof of your mouth just behind your top teeth.

/ ʒ /

From this position you should move your tongue down a little and use your voice to make the sound / ʒ /.

2   Listen to the pairs of words in 1 again, and repeat them paying attention to the pronunciation of the two sounds.

Work with a partner. You should say any of the words in 1 and your partner should point to the word that he or she hears. Practise again any words that your partner cannot understand correctly.

3 | T.14.1.B. | Listen to the tongue-twisters below. Underline the / j / sounds like this ____ and the / dʒ / sounds like this ∿∿. Remember that there may be some 'extra' / j / sounds before the sound / uː /.

a. In his youth, Jerry Josephs, the New York millionaire, used to play jazz on a huge German tuba.
b. Julian Jones is jealous of Eunice's Jaguar, but Eunice Jones is jealous of Jason's jacuzzi, and Jason Jones is jealous of Julian's yacht.
c. That fabulous jade unicorn is the most beautiful Japanese statue in any European museum.
d. Journalist Jane Young stupidly damaged George Joyce's new yellow jeep on the edge of the bridge.

⎯0

Practise saying the tongue-twisters first slowly and then gradually faster and faster.

---

Do this exercise after the Reading on pages 81–3 of the Student's Book.

## 2 Revision of vowel sounds – / e /, / ɪ /, / iː /, / eɪ /, and / aɪ /
( All Nationalities )

1 All of these words come from the newspaper articles on pages 81–83 of the Student's Book. Can you remember what they all mean?

| Kennedy | immediate | naked |
| recent | find | dead |
| chief | sign | beach |
| discovered | died | death |
| pray | strike | office |
| disease | described | said |
| visit | related | assassinated |
| biography | peace | life |

2 Look at the vowel sounds marked and put the words into the correct columns.

| / e / | / ɪ / |
| --- | --- |
|  |  |
|  |  |
|  |  |
|  |  |

| / iː / | / eɪ / |
| --- | --- |
|  |  |
|  |  |
|  |  |
|  |  |

| / aɪ / |
| --- |
|  |
|  |
|  |
|  |

| T.14.2. | Listen and check your answers.

3 Listen again and practise any words that you put into the wrong column.

---

Do this exercise after the Listening on page 84 of the Student's Book.

## 3 Revision of vowel sounds – / ɒ /, / ʌ /, / ɜː /, / ɔː /, / əʊ /, and / aʊ /
( All Nationalities )

All of these words come from the listening on page

84 of the Student's Book | T.39 |. Can you remember what they all mean?

| divorce | common |
| court | husband |
| couple | important |
| intolerable | broken |
| become | flowers |
| home | hurt |
| about | grown |
| emotion | courage |
| circumstances | cause |
| dishonest | conservative |
| however | personally |
| front | suffer |

Look at the vowel sounds marked and put the words into the correct columns.

| / ɒ / | / ʌ / |
|-------|-------|
| common | |

| / ɜː / | / ɔː / |
|--------|--------|
| | divorce |

| / əʊ / | / aʊ / |
|--------|--------|
| | |

**T.14.3.** Listen and check your answers.

Listen again and practise any words that you put into the wrong column.

## ● Connected speech

Do this exercise after the reading about the Shipbuilders' Strike on page 78 of the Student's Book.

## 4 Reading aloud

1 **T.14.4.** Listen to the first paragraph of the newspaper article from page 78 of the Student's Book. Mark the stressed syllables with a box □.

    □    □    □    □
The bitter strike over pay and redundancies has

  □  □    □    □
now lasted over eight weeks. Shipbuilders have told

their leaders to 'fight to the end' to stop dockyards

from closing and two thousand of their men losing

their jobs.

2 Listen again and answer these questions.

   a. Which words become very weak?
   b. Are there any words where the last sound links on to the beginning of the next word?

     **Example** strike‿over . . .

   c. Are there any words that have an extra sound between them to link them together?

     **Example** pay‿/ j /‿and . . .

3 Read the passage together with the tape, paying attention to **stress**, **weak forms**, and **linking**.

4 Look at the rest of the article on page 78 of the Student's Book. Decide with a partner where the **stress**, **weak forms**, and **word linking** come. Practise reading it aloud in turns, checking each other's pronunciation.

# ● Intonation and sentence stress

## 5 Showing disbelief

1 **T.14.5.A.** Listen to the following dialogues. Who does **not** believe what Sally said? How does the stress and intonation show this?

Notice the stress and intonation. To show disbelief there is a special stress on *said* and the intonation goes **down** like this:

She said she had a headache.

Whereas the intonation in the ordinary type of sentence is like this:

She said she had a headache.

2 Listen again and repeat the replies, paying attention to the intonation.

3 **T.14.5.B.** Now listen to the following dialogues. Mark the dialogues like this* if you think **B** does not believe what he is reporting.

a. **A** Does Judith like her new job?
   **B** She said she liked it.

b. **A** How was Paul's dinner party?
   **B** Everyone said they enjoyed it.*

c. **A** Where did Peter get that £10 note?
   **B** He said he'd found it.

d. **A** Can you remind Helen about my £20?
   **B** She said that she had already paid you.

e. **A** Why didn't Phil come to the lesson yesterday?
   **B** He said he was too busy.

f. **A** How's Mandy's diet going?
   **B** She said she had lost 5 kilos.

g. **A** Has David found my book yet?
   **B** No, but he said he'd looked everywhere.

h. **A** What's happening between Linda and Tony?
   **B** I don't know, but she said she wasn't interested in him.

4 Write six things that people have told you recently, three that you believe and three that you do not believe.

**Examples**

*A woman at work told me that her husband had just been promoted again.*

*My brother said last night that he hadn't been smoking.*

Tell your partner about the things that you have written down in conversations like this. **You should make it clear from your intonation whether or not you believed what you were told.**

**You**

A woman at work told me that her husband had just been promoted again.

**Your partner**

And you didn't believe her?

Yes, I've heard that he's very good at his job.

*or*

**You**

My brother said last night that he hadn't been smoking.

**Your partner**

But you didn't believe him?

No, because his breath smelt of smoke.

---

## 6 Revision

1  **T.14.6.**  Listen to the following pairs of sentences. The words are identical, but the intonation is different. Listen and write down how you think the message is different in each case. (You can make your notes in your own language if you prefer.)

a.  i.  'I've just bought a lovely skirt in the sale.'

'<u>Really</u>?'

_____

ii.  'I've just bought a lovely skirt in the sale.'

'<u>Really</u>?'

_____

b.  i.  That book you lent me was <u>quite funny</u>.

_____

ii.  That book you lent me was <u>quite funny</u>.

_____

c.  i.  'Do you enjoy cooking?'

'<u>Mmm</u>.'

_____

ii.  'Do you enjoy cooking?

'<u>Mmm</u>.'

_____

d.  i.  You've met my parents, <u>haven't you</u>?

_____

ii.  You've met my parents, <u>haven't you</u>?

_____

e.  i.  'What did your husband think of your new hairstyle?'

'<u>He said he liked it</u>.'

_____

ii.  'What did your husband think of your new hairstyle?'

'<u>He said he liked it</u>.'

_____

2  Listen and repeat the sentences, paying attention to the intonation. Practise reading the dialogues with a partner.

# ● Word focus

## 7 Adverbs – revision

1 Fill in the empty spaces below. Use a dictionary to help you.

| noun | adjective | adverb |
|------|-----------|--------|
| *anger* | angry | _____ |
| _____ | _____ | proudly |
| sarcasm | _____ | _____ |
| _____ | _____ | shyly |
| _____ | tactful | _____ |
| apology | _____ | _____ |
| hesitation | _____ | _____ |
| _____ | _____ | wittily |
| _____ | cheerful | _____ |
| generosity | _____ | _____ |
| _____ | stupid | _____ |
| _____ | polite | _____ |

2 **T.14.7.** Listen and check your answers.

🔑

3 Listen to the groups of words again. Sometimes the stress pattern is different in the adjective from the stress pattern in the noun. Mark these adjectives with a ∗.

🔑

4 Choose one of the adverbs above, but do not tell the rest of the class what it is. Now follow one of the instructions below **in the manner of the adverb**. The other students must guess what your adverb is.

Ask to borrow a small amount of money from your teacher.

Persuade one of the other students to come out for a drink with you after the lesson.

Explain the difference between an adjective and adverb to the rest of the class.

Point out to your teacher that he or she has a hole in his or her shoes.

Offer to help one of the other students with his or her homework.

Advise one of the other students about how to improve his or her health.

## 8 Words with different suffixes

1 Look at these groups of words and fill in the gaps.

a. **-tion nouns**

organize    *organization*

pronounce  _____

describe    _____

explain     _____

b. **-ous adjectives**

fame       *famous*

disaster   _____

hilarity   _____

ambition   _____

c. **-ed adjectives**

frighten   *frightened*

terrify    _____

fascinate  _____

tire       _____

d. **-ness nouns**

clever     *cleverness*

mean       _____

neat       _____

polite     _____

e. **-sion nouns**

revise     *revision*

decide     _____

invade     _____

explode    _____

f. **-less adjectives**

care       *careless*

price      _____

use        _____

worth      _____

g. *-ing adjectives*

boil     *boiling*

freeze

disgust

worry

h. *-able adjectives*

reason     *reasonable*

enjoy

believe

profit

⚷—O

2   **T.14.8.**   Can you remember how all of these suffixes are pronounced? Listen and check.

3   How many more words can you remember with the same suffixes? You can look back through your Student's Book to help you.

# ● Everyday English

## 9 Revision dialogues

1   **T.14.9.**   Listen to the dialogues and fill in the gaps.

A (a.) _____ Classified. Can I help you?

B Hello. Yes, I'd like to put an ad in your For Sale section.

A What's the wording?

B (b.) _____ for sale. F registration (c.) _____ and taxed. (d.) _____ condition. (e.) _____ or nearest offer. Ring (f.) _____ after (g.) _____ .

C Reach (h.) _____ Londoners per week. Sell your house or flat in Time Out. 20 words for (i.) _____ or a (j.) _____ box for (k.) _____ .

D I say, this looks nice.

E Oh yes?

D London (l.) _____ . Spacious sunny top floor flat. (m.) _____ by (n.) _____ 3 bedrooms and kitchen/diner.

E Oh.

D Oh, but it's (o.) _____ . That's rather a lot, isn't it?

F Fancy a pair of Ray-Ban sunglasses for just (p.) _____ ? Come to the (q.) _____ Fashion sale at 259 King's (r.) _____ London (s.) _____ . Open Monday to Saturday (t.) _____ to (u.) _____ . But hurry. Sale ends on the (v.) _____ .

⚷—O

2   Listen again and read the dialogues at the same time as the tape. Practise until you are happy with your pronunciation. Now read with a partner.

85

# KEY

## THE PHONEMIC ALPHABET

### 1 Vowels (1)

3  T.0.1.B.

a. /ɒ/    h. /ʊ/    o. /iː/
<u>ho</u>t     w<u>oo</u>l    f<u>ee</u>l

b. /ɪ/    i. /ʊ/    p. /ɪ/
h<u>i</u>t     p<u>u</u>ll    f<u>i</u>ll

c. /uː/    j. /ɪ/
r<u>u</u>de    p<u>i</u>ll    q. b<u>oo</u>t

d. /iː/    k. /ɪ/    r. /ɔː/
r<u>ea</u>d    s<u>i</u>t     b<u>ou</u>ght

e. /ʊ/    l. /iː/    s. /iː/
g<u>oo</u>d    s<u>ea</u>t    b<u>ea</u>t

f. /ɒ/    m. /ɔː/    t. /ɪ/
G<u>o</u>d    f<u>a</u>ll    b<u>i</u>t

g. /ɔː/    n. /uː/
w<u>a</u>ll    f<u>oo</u>l

### 2 Vowels (2)

3  T.0.2.B.

a. man / æ /    g. heard / ɜː /
b. men / e /     h. hard / ɑː /
c. fast / ɑː /    i. pass / ɑː /
d. first / ɜː /    j. purse / ɜː /
e. head / e /    k. run / ʌ /
f. had / æ /     l. ran / æ /

4  a. / ɑː / / ə /    g. / ʌ / / ə /
father        butter

b. / ʌ / / ə /    h. / ɒ / / ə /
mother      chocolate

c. / ɪ / / ə /    i. / ɪ / / ə /
sister        singer

d. / ʌ / / ə /    j. / æ / / ə /
brother      actress

e. / ɒ / / ɪ /    k. / iː / / ə /
orange       teacher

f. / ʊ / / ə /    l. / ɒ / / ə /
sugar        doctor

### 3 Consonants

3  a. jump    g. that
   b. your    h. bank
   c. cheap    i. think
   d. through    j. lunch

e. orange    k. these
f. young     l. church

### 4 Diphthongs (1)

2  T.0.4.B.

a. pay / eɪ /    h. Wales / eɪ /
b. voice / ɔɪ /    i. case / eɪ /
c. loud / aʊ /    j. try / aɪ /
d. grey / eɪ /    k. coin / ɔɪ /
e. die / aɪ /     l. high / aɪ /
f. noise / ɔɪ /    m. flower / aʊ /
g. house / aʊ /    n. weigh / eɪ /

### 5 Diphthongs (2)

3  a. bear / beə /    e. they / ðeɪ /
     beer / bɪə /     though / ðəʊ /
     bay / beɪ /      there / ðeə /

b. toy / tɔɪ /    f. I'll / aɪl /
   tie / taɪ /      oil / ɔɪl /
   toe / təʊ /     owl / aʊl /

c. roll / rəʊl /    g. dear / dɪə /
   real / rɪəl /     day / deɪ /
   rail / reɪl /     die / daɪ /

d. how / haʊ /    h. show / ʃəʊ /
   hair / heə /     share / ʃeə /
   high / haɪ /     shy / ʃaɪ /

---

# UNIT 1

## 1

2  T.1.1.B.

| / s / | / z / | / ɪz / |
|-------|-------|--------|
| likes | owns | watches |
| works | goes | kisses |
| takes | remembers | rises |
| visits | comes | washes |
| picks | | closes |

3  RULES
   a. / ɪz /    b. / s /    c. / z /

4  / z /         / ɪz /
suburbs     chances

    / ɪz /          / z /
houses      bedrooms

    / z /           / z /
gardens     hours

    / s /          / ɪz /
weeks       buses

    / s /          / s /
pets         sports

    / z /          / z /
children's    miles

## 2

1  T.1.2.A.

The *s* at the *beginning* of words is always pronounced / s / not / z / (except *sh*).

3  T.1.2.B.

a. I speak Spanish, but unfortunately, I don't speak Swedish.
b. Steve speaks very slowly, doesn't he?
c. On Sunday, it was snowing in Scandinavia, Switzerland and Spain.
d. He has stopped playing sports and started smoking.
e. In her spare time, Stephanie plays squash and goes swimming.

## 3

3  T.1.3.C.

a. ✓     f. ✓
b. ✗     g. ✓
c. ✗     h. ✗
d. ✓     i. ✓
e. ✗     j. ✗

T.1.3.D.

a. I'm studying at a language school in London.
b. I'm staying with a very nice woman with two children.
c. Her husband's working abroad.
d. He's earning a lot of money, I think.
e. He's not enjoying himself very much.

f. His wife's trying to keep busy.
g. She's learning Italian.
h. I'm helping her.
i. And she's helping me with my English.
j. We're having a great time!

## 4

1 | T.1.4.A. |

A Do you like sport?
B Yes I do, I love it!
A Which sports do you play?
B Oh, I don't play any myself, but I watch them all on TV!

The **weak form** is used in the questions.
The **strong form** is used in the short answer.
(The above are also true for other auxiliary verbs that have weak forms.)

3 | T.1.4.C. |

a. . . . – Do you go running?
   – No, I don't.
b. . . . – Do you play tennis?
   – No, I don't.
c. . . . – Do you play basketball?
   – No, I don't.
d. . . . – Do you go cycling?
   – No, I don't.
e. . . . – Do you go riding?
   – No, I don't.
f. . . . – Do you play golf?
   – No, I don't.
g. . . . – Do you go skiing?
   – No, I don't.
h. . . . – Do you go windsurfing?
   – No, I don't.
i. . . . – Do you play volleyball?
   – No, I don't.

## 5

1 | T.1.5.A. |

a. A Paul McCartney lives in a two-bedroom house!
   B *Does he?*
b. A Linda McCartney has a seventeen-year-old daughter!
   B *Does she?*
c. A The McCartneys are all vegetarians!
   B *Are they?*
d. A Paul McCartney knows how to bake bread!
   B *Does he?*
e. A Linda drives a very small car!
   B *Does she?*
f. A Linda does all the cooking herself!
   B *Does she?*
g. A Paul and Linda both love football!
   B *Do they?*
h. A Linda much prefers living in the country!
   B *Does she?*
i. A In the evening the McCartneys usually just watch TV!
   B *Do they?*

## 6

1 | T.1.6.B. |

a. Excuse me, where can I get stamps?
b. Excuse me, where's the nearest post office?
c. Excuse me, where's the nearest bank?
d. What time does it open?
e. What time does it close?
f. Where can I find cheap accommodation?
g. How much does a single room cost?
h. What's the address?

i. What's the telephone number?

The main stress is on the last word (or compound word).
The intonation goes **down**. This is the most usual intonation for *Wh-* questions.

## 7

2 Syllables with the vowel / ə / are **never** stressed.

## 8

1 | T.1.8.A. |

a. A What's your address, Miss Norman?
   B *57 Fawnbrake Avenue, S.E. 24.*
   A 57 Fawnbrake Avenue . . . how do you spell Fawnbrake?
   B F–A–W–N–B–R–A–K–E
   A And you said London SE 24?
   B That's right.
   A And have you got a telephone number?
   B Yes, its *01* for London and then *354–3445.*
   A Thank you very much.

b. A Can you give me your address, Mr Wood?
   B It's *64 Brynland Road, Bristol.*
   A And how do you spell Brynland?
   B B–R–Y–N–L–A–N–D
   A And it's Bristol, you said?
   B That's right – the phone number is *0273* for Bristol and then *496211.*
   A Thank you very much.

c. A Can you give me your address, Miss Bailey?
   B Certainly, it's *15 Welhome Road, Oxford.*
   A 15 Welholme Road . . . Oxford . . . how exactly do you spell Welholme?
   B W–E–L–H–O–L–M–E
   A And your phone number?
   B *Oxford 57233.*

d. **A** Could I have your address and phone number please, Mr. Crocker?
   **B** *95 Leigham Street . . .*
   **A** How do you spell Leigham?
   **B** L–E–I–G–H–A–M
   **A** Thank you . . . is that in London?
   **B** Yes, *London NW10 . . .* the phone number's *686–3434.*
   **A** Thanks very much.

---

# UNIT 2

## 1

1   T.2.1.A.

| / v / | / w / |
| --- | --- |
| Conser*v*ative | *w*ants |
| producti*v*ity | *w*ill |
| belie*v*es | *p*ower |
| *v*ery | *w*eapons |
| twel*v*e | *w*orld |
| tele*v*ision | *w*ork |
|  | t*w*elve |
|  | *w*atching |
|  | *o*ne |
|  | (and *w*orks) |

3   *wr* is always pronounced / r /.
    *wh* + *o* is pronounced / h / but
    *wh* + *a*, *e*, *i* is pronounced / w /.

## 2

1   T.2.2.A.

**Bob**   *Would* you like to dance?
**Anna** No, thanks.
**Bob**   *Do* you like cocktails?
**Anna** Yes, I do.
**Bob**   *Would* you like something to drink?
**Anna** No, thanks.
**Bob**   *Do* you like hamburgers?
**Anna** Yes, I do.
**Bob**   *Would* you like something to eat?
**Anna** No, thanks.
**Bob**   *Would* you like a cigarette?
**Anna** No, thanks.
**Bob**   *Do* you like this music?

**Anna** Yes, I do.
**Bob**   *Do you* like the disc jockey?
**Anna** He's *my boyfriend.*

The **weak form** is used in the question. The **strong form** is used in the short answer. This is also true for other auxiliary verbs that have a weak form.

## 3

1   T.2.3.A.

**A** *Cagney and Lacey*'s on BBC 1, isn't it?
**B** Yes, that's right, it's on at 9.25.

*at* is pronounced / ət / in the dialogue. This is the **weak form**.

3   T.2.3.C.

a. *Cagney and Lacey*'s on BBC 1, isn't it?
   . . .
   Yes, that's right, it's on at 9.25.
b. *Gardener's World*'s on BBC 2, isn't it?
   . . .
   Yes, that's right, it's on at 8.35.
c. *Postman Pat*'s on BBC 1, isn't it?
   . . .
   Yes, that's right, it's on at 1.45.
d. *Countdown*'s on Channel 4, isn't it?
   . . .
   Yes, that's right, it's on at 5.30.
e. *The Big Shot*'s on Channel 4 too, isn't it?
   . . .
   Yes, that's right, it's on at 11.15.
f. *Family Fortunes* is on ITV, isn't it?
   . . .
   Yes, that's right, it's on at 7.00.

g. *Dangermouse*'s on ITV too, isn't it?
   . . .
   Yes, that's right, it's on at 4.20.
h. *Newsnight*'s on BBC 2, isn't it?
   . . .
   Yes, that's right, it's on at 10.25.

## 4

1   a. 6    d. 5    g. 6
    b. 7    e. 6    h. 7
    c. 7    f. 9

2   T.2.4.

a. How *often do you* go skiing?
b. *Would you like to* borrow *this* magazine?
c. *Is there* anything good *on* television tonight?
d. What time*'s it on?*
e. I *like going out for* meals.
f. I*'d like to go out for* a meal.
g. *Are you any* good *at* athletics?
h. I*'m not very good at* running.

3   *to* is pronounced / tə /; *for* is pronounced / fə / or / fər / before a vowel (as in f. above); *are you . . .?* is pronounced / əjʊ / or / əjə /. These are all **weak forms**.

## 5

1   T.2.5.A.

– Do you like *English music?*
– Yeah, it's great!
– Would you like *to hear some?*
– Yes, please!
– Do you like *English books?*
– Yeah, they're great!
– Would you like *to borrow some?*
– Yes, please!
– Do you like *English people?*
– Yeah, they're great!
– Would you like *to meet some?*
– Yes, please!
– Do you like *English food?*

– Yeah, it's great!
– Would you like *to try some*?
– Er . . . no thanks . . .

The intonation starts very high. This is so that the visitor sounds interested and enthusiastic. If the intonation is flat, then the speaker will probably sound bored or impolite.

3  T.2.5.C.

Do you like English music?
. . .
Would you like to hear some?
. . .
Do you like English books?
. . .
Would you like to borrow some?
. . .
Do you like English people?
. . .
Would you like to meet some?
. . .
Do you like English food?
. . .
Would you like to try some?
. . .

## 6

1  T.2.6.

a. ◼↴   e. ◼↗   i. ◼↗

b. ◼↗   f. ◼↗   j. ◼↴

c. ◼↴   g. ◼↗   k. ◼↴

d. ◼↗   h. ◼↴

## 7

T.2.7.

a. Do you like American films? ◼↗

b. Where would you like to go ◼↴
   this evening?

c. Would you like to see a play? ◼↗

d. Would you like to watch the ◼↗
   news?

e. What sort of books do you ◼↴
   read?

f. Do you like cooking? ◼↗

g. Do you play tennis? ◼↗

h. Would you like something ◼↗
   to drink?

i. What would you like for dinner? ◼↴

j. Which newspaper do you read? ◼↴

2  Questions with the answer *yes* or *no* go **up** at the end.

Questions starting with a *Wh*-word (e.g. *What*, *Where*, *Which*, *Who*, *How* etc.) go **down** at the end.

## 8

1  The stress is always on the second to last syllable in words ending in *-tion* and *-sion*. *-sion* is pronounced / ʒən /; *-tion* is pronounced / ʃən /.

## 9

2  T.2.9.

a. cartoon
b. comedy
c. comedian
d. documentary
e. programme
f. quiz
g. theatre
h. western

## 10

1  T.2.10.

a. – What's another way of saying 2.00 a.m.?
   . . .
   – Two o'clock in the morning.

b. – What's another way of saying 6.35?
   . . .
   – Twenty-five to seven.

c. – What's another way of saying 7.10?
   . . .
   – Ten past seven.

d. – What's another way of saying 4.00 p.m.?
   . . .
   – Four o'clock in the afternoon.

e. – What's another way of saying 9.45?
   . . .
   – Quarter to ten.

f. – What's another way of saying 1.55?
   . . .
   – Five to two.

g. – What's another way of saying midnight?
   . . .
   – Twelve o'clock at night.

h. – What's another way of saying 3.15?
   . . .
   – Quarter past three.

i. – What's another way of saying 8.30 p.m.?
   . . .
   – Half past eight in the evening.

j. – What's another way of saying 9.40 a.m.?
   . . .
   – Twenty to ten in the morning.

# UNIT 3

## 2

1 | T.3.2.A. |

| / t / | / d / | / ɪd / |
| --- | --- | --- |
| helped | offered | started |
| reached | saved | needed |
| missed | lived | invited |
| looked | discovered | waited |
| asked | called | |
| jumped | tried | |

2   a. / ɪd /    b. / t /    c. / d /

3 | T.3.2.B. |

a. / ɪd /      c. / t /
   / ɪd /        / ɪd /
   / d /         / d /
b. / t /      d. / ɪd /
   / d /         / d /
   / t /         / d /

## 3

1 | T.3.3. |

a. Their teenage children *were having a party*.
b. Their daughter Sue *was dancing on the table*.
c. Their son Philip *was watching a Kung Fu video*.
d. Their son Peter *was smoking his father's cigars*.
e. Philip's girlfriend *was lying asleep on the floor*.
f. Sue's boyfriend *was drinking Mr Bailey's whisky*.
g. Peter's girlfriend *was phoning her brother in Australia*.
h. Two of Philip's friends *were playing poker*.
i. Two of Sue's friends *were kissing on the sofa*.

3   *was* is pronounced / wəz /; *were* is pronounced / wə / (before a vowel it is pronounced / wər / e.g. *were expecting* / wər ɪks'pektɪŋ /).

## 4

1,2 | T.3.4.A. |

a. A Last summer we hitchhiked all the way to Turkey.
   B *Did you?*
b. A Yes, and it only took three days.
   B *Did it?*
c. C We were in Hawaii this time last week.
   D *Were you?*
d. C Mmm. It was absolutely fantastic.
   D *Was it?*
e. E John and Vera had a lovely holiday in Corfu.
   F *Did they?*
f. E Yes, and John took some lovely photographs.
   F *Did he?*
g. G We spent our holidays in Britain this year.
   H *Did you?*
h. G Yes, but it was more expensive than going abroad.
   H *Was it?*
i. I June and her husband went to Scotland to play golf last week.
   J *Did they?*
j. I Yes. June had a wonderful time.
   J *Did she?*

a. Did you (I)
b. Did it? (I)
c. Were you? (I)
d. Was it? (I)
e. Did they? (U)
f. Did he? (U)
g. Did you? (I)
h. Was it? (I)
i. Did they? (U)
j. Did she? (U)

4 | T.3.4.C. |

a. A I went to New Zealand for my holidays this year.
   . . .
   B Did you?
b. A My son went to the Cannes film festival last year.
   . . .
   B Did he?
c. A When we were in Greece the temperature was over 40°.
   . . .
   B Was it?
d. A We were in Rio for the carnival last year.
   . . .
   B Were you?
e. A My husband and I met on holiday in Spain.
   . . .
   B Did you?
f. A Some friends of mine drove all the way to Istanbul.
   . . .
   B Did they?
g. A Vienna was terribly expensive.
   . . .
   B Was it?
h. A We thought Portugal was very cheap.
   . . .
   B Did you?
i. A The people in Moscow were very friendly.
   . . .
   B Were they?

## 5

1 | T.3.5. |

     □
On the fourteenth day of
  □     □     □     □
January nineteen seventy-eight,
     □     □
Mrs Brewin was working in her
  □
garden.
   □    □      □
Her cat, Henry, was playing

around her.
  □      □      □
It climbed a tree in the garden
     □     □
and couldn't get down, so she

□ □
called the Fire Brigade.

□ □
While she was waiting for them

□ □
to arrive, she offered him some

□ □ □
fish to try to get him down.

2 The words which are **stressed** are the ones which give the **message** in the sentence e.g. **nouns** (*January*, *Brewin* etc.); **verbs** (*working*, *playing* etc.) and sometimes **adjectives**.

Words like **prepositions** (*on*, *in* etc.), **articles** (*a*, *the*) and **auxiliary verbs** (*was*, etc.) are not *usually* stressed.

# 6

1   1 ● ●          2 ● ● ●

famous            curious
jealous           dangerous
precious          generous
                  poisonous

3 ● ● ●          4 ● ● ● ●

delicious         ridiculous
disastrous        hilarious
religious

# 7

1,2   T.3.7.

money
credit card
finance company
earns
borrowed
loan
bankruptcy
monthly statement

# 8

1   T.3.8.A.

ten p
one pound
ten pounds
a hundred pounds
a thousand pounds
fifty-five p
five pounds fifty
fifty-five pounds
five hundred and fifty pounds
five thousand five hundred and
   fifty pounds
ninety-nine p
nine pounds ninety-nine
ninety-nine pounds ninety-nine
nine hundred and ninety-nine
   pounds ninety-nine
nine thousand nine hundred and
   ninety-nine pounds
   ninety-nine

2   T.3.8.B.

a.  A Excuse me for asking, but how much did your bag cost?
    . . .
    B It was £19.99 actually.

b.  A Excuse me, but how much did you pay for your gloves?
    . . .
    B They were £9.95 actually.

c.  A Excuse me, would you mind telling me how much your tie cost?
    . . .
    B It was £12.95 actually.

d.  A Excuse me for asking, but how much did your walkman cost?
    . . .
    B It was £39.95 actually.

e.  A Excuse me, would you mind telling me how much your earrings cost?
    . . .
    B They were £13.50 actually.

f.  A Excuse me, would you mind telling me how much your shoes cost?
    . . .
    B They were £27.95 actually.

g.  A Excuse me for asking, but how much did your computer cost?
    . . .
    B It was £399 actually.

h.  A Excuse me, but how much did you pay for your typewriter?
    . . .
    B It was £275 actually.

# 9

1   T.3.9.A.

10th . . . the 10th . . . the 10th of May . . . the 10th of May 1983

3rd . . . the 3rd . . . the 3rd of March . . . the 3rd of March 1934

13th . . . the 13th . . . the 13th of December . . . the 13th of December 1793

12th . . . the 12th . . . the 12th of February . . . the 12th of February 1903

24th . . . the 24th . . . the 24th of July . . . the 24th of July 1963

30th . . . the 30th . . . the 30th of September . . . the 30th of September 1833

3   T.3.9.B.

a.  Marie Antoinette was born on the *2nd of November 1755*.
b.  Napoleon Bonaparte was born on the *15th of August 1769*.
c.  Michelangelo Buonarotti was born on the *6th of March 1475*.
d.  Agatha Christie was born on the *15th of September 1890*.
e.  Greta Garbo was born on the *18th of September 1905*.
f.  Mikhail Gorbachev was born on the *2nd of March 1931*.
g.  Karl Marx was born on the *5th of May 1818*.
h.  Marilyn Monroe was born on the *1st of June 1926*.
i.  Pablo Picasso was born on the *25th of October 1881*.
j.  Elvis Presley was born on the *8th of January 1938*.
k.  William Shakespeare was born on the *23rd of April 1564*.
l.  Margaret Thatcher was born on the *13th of October 1925*.

## UNIT 4

### 1

2 **T.4.1.B.**

   a. cold
   b. gun
   c. call
   d. got
   e. gold
   f. what
   g. cot
   h. girl
   i. wall
   j. wide

### 2

1 **T.4.2.**

   a. *Could* you tell me the time?
   b. *Would* you lend me your pencil?
   c. *Could* you do me a favour?
   d. *Could* you take this upstairs with you?
   e. *Would* you fetch my glasses from the kitchen?
   f. *Could* I borrow some money?
   g. *Would* you help me to carry this?
   h. *Would* you read this through?

### 3

1,2 **T.4.3.**

   a. 8     d. 8
   b. 8     e. 10
   c. 6     f. 9

   a. *Shall I close the* window *or the door*?
   b. *I'll go to the* shops *for you*.
   c. *Shall I turn the* television *on*?
   d. *I'll drive you to the* airport *tomorrow*.
   e. *I'll make you a nice hot cup of* coffee.
   f. *Shall I open the* red wine *or the white*?

2 **T.4.4.A.**

   1.A P     2.A P
   1.B R     2.B R

3.A R     5.A R
3.B P     5.B P
4.A R     6.A P
4.B P     6.B R

4 **T.4.4.C.**

In sentences b. d. and h. you should not respond because the request was not polite.

### 5

**T.4.5.**

   a. A a beer.
      . . .
      Do you think you could bring me a beer please?
      B Certainly.

   b. A a menu.
      . . .
      Do you think you could bring me a menu please?
      B Certainly.

   c. A some matches.
      . . .
      Do you think you could bring me some matches please?
      B Certainly.

   d. A an ashtray.
      . . .
      Do you think you could bring me an ashtray please?
      B Certainly.

   e. A a hamburger.
      . . .
      Do you think you could bring me a hamburger please?
      B Certainly.

   f. A a coffee.
      . . .
      Do you think you could bring me a coffee please?
      B Certainly.

   g. A a brandy.
      . . .
      Do you think you could bring me a brandy please?
      B Certainly.

   h. A the bill.
      . . .

Do you think you could bring me the bill please?
B Certainly.

### 6

1 **T.4.6.A.**

   1. A Did you like Portugal?
      B Yes! I found Portuguese people very friendly.

   2. A Did you like Switzerland?
      B Yes . . . but I found Swiss people very serious.

3 **T.4.6.C.**

   a. A Did you like Czechoslovakia?
      . . .
      B Yes, I found Czech people very sociable.

   b. A Did you like Norway?
      . . .
      B Yes, I found Norwegian people very helpful.

   c. A Did you like Sweden?
      . . .
      B Yes*, but I found Swedish people very reserved.

   d. A Did you like Australia?
      . . .
      B Yes*, but I found Australian people very noisy.

   e. A Did you like Italy?
      . . .
      B Yes, I found Italian people very good fun.

   f. A Did you like Brazil?
      . . .
      B Yes, I found Brazilian people very open.

   g. A Did you like Japan?
      . . .
      B Yes*, but I found Japanese people very quiet.

h. A Did you like Hungary?

. . .

   B Yes, I found Hungarian people very hospitable.

\* In these sentences the speaker is *unsure*. In the others he is enthusiastic.

## 7

1    T.4.7.

a. upset
b. advertise
c. offensive
d. voluntary
e. advertisement
f. luggage
g. hitchhike
h. complain
i. commercial
j. journey
k. nervous
l. vehicle

## 8

2  Egypt          Czechoslovakia

   Iran           Switzerland

   Japan          Israel

   Ireland        Saudi Arabia

   China          Belgium

   Brazil         Iraq

   Portugal       Hungary

   Vietnam        Finland

   Norway         Canada

   Poland

5    T.4.8.B.

a. A Where's São Paolo?

. . .

   B Yes, that's right. It's in Brazil.

b. A Where's Budapest?

. . .

   B Yes, that's right. It's in Hungary.

c. A Where's Harbin?

. . .

   B Yes, that's right. It's in China.

d. A Where's Faro?

. . .

   B Yes, that's right. It's in Portugal.

e. A Where's Baghdad?

. . .

   B Yes, that's right. It's in Iraq.

f. A Where's Hanoi?

. . .

   B Yes, that's right. It's in Vietnam.

g. A Where's Gdansk?

. . .

   B Yes, that's right. It's in Poland.

h. A Where's Jaffa?

. . .

   B Yes, that's right. It's in Israel.

i. A Where's Antwerp?

. . .

   B Yes, that's right. It's in Belgium.

j. A Where's Cork?

. . .

   B Yes, that's right. It's in Ireland.

k. A Where's Riyadh?

. . .

   B Yes, that's right. It's in Saudi Arabia.

## 9

3    T.4.9.

| 1. -ian | 2. -ish |
|---------|---------|
| Egyptian | Irish |
| Iranian | Polish |
| Brazilian | Finnish |
| Norwegian | |
| Hungarian | |
| Belgian | |
| Canadian | |

| 3. -ese | 4. -i |
|---------|-------|
| Japanese | Israeli |
| Chinese | Saudi |
| Portuguese | Iraqi |
| Vietnamese | |

| 5. other |
|----------|
| Czech |
| Swiss |

The adjectives ending in *-ian* have the stress on the second to last syllable.
The adjectives ending in *-ish* have the stress on the first syllable.
The adjectives ending in *-ese* have the stress on the last syllable.
The adjectives ending in *-i* have the stress on the second to last syllable.

# UNIT 5

## 1

1    T.5.1.A.

a. *I* go to the baker's and buy a loaf. (incorrect)
b. *I* go to the post office. (incorrect)
c. *I'll* buy him a book. (correct)
d. *I* buy her a doll. (incorrect)
e. *He'll* be forty-five next week. (correct)
f. *I* have a steak please. (incorrect)
g. *We'll* go and visit him. (correct)
h. *I'll* give you my number. (correct)

4  **Baker's** – bread; rolls.
   **Butcher's** – steak; sausages.
   **Chemist's** – aspirin; shampoo.

**Greengrocer's** – bananas; tomatoes.
**Off Licence** – vodka; whisky.
**Tobacconist's** – matches; cigarettes.

---

**T.5.1.D.**

a. A We haven't got any bread left.
   . . .
   B Okay, I'll go to the baker's and buy some.

b. A We haven't got any cigarettes left.
   . . .
   B Okay, I'll go to the tobacconist's and buy some.

c. A We haven't got any whisky left.
   . . .
   B Okay, I'll go to the off licence and buy some.

d. A We haven't got any bananas left.
   . . .
   B Okay, I'll go to the greengrocer's and buy some.

e. A We haven't got any steak left.
   . . .
   B Okay, I'll go to the butcher's and buy some.

f. A We haven't got any aspirin left.
   . . .
   B Okay, I'll go to the chemist's and buy some.

g. A We haven't got any matches left.
   . . .
   B Okay, I'll go to the tobacconist's and buy some.

h. A We haven't got any tomatoes left.
   . . .
   B Okay, I'll go to the greengrocer's and buy some.

i. A We haven't got any shampoo left.
   . . .
   B Okay, I'll go to the chemist's and buy some.

j. A We haven't got any vodka left.
   . . .
   B Okay, I'll go to the off licence and buy some.

k. A We haven't got any rolls left.
   . . .
   B Okay, I'll go to the baker's and buy some.

l. A We haven't got any sausages left.
   . . .
   B Okay, I'll go to the butcher's and buy some.

## 2

2 **T.5.2.B.**

| | | |
|---|---|---|
| a. /ɒ/ | e. /ɒ/ | i. /ɒ/ |
| b. /ɒ/ | f. /əʊ/ | j. /əʊ/ |
| c. /əʊ/ | g. /əʊ/ | k. /əʊ/ |
| d. /ɒ/ | h. /əʊ/ | l. /ɒ/ |

4 **T.5.2.E.**

a. A John! There's Joan on the phone.
   B Oh no! Not Joan!

b. C It's going to snow!
   D Oh . . . I won't go home then . . .
   C No. . . ?

c. E Okay then! I'm going!
   F Oh . . . oh . . . please don't go Polly!

d. G He won't show me those photos, you know!
   H Why won't he show you them?
   G I don't know!

## 3

1 **T.5.3.A.**

And now here's the weather forecast for the next twenty-four hours for the whole of England, Wales, Scotland and Northern Ireland.

A **vowel sound** comes at the beginning of the second word.

1 **T.5.3.B.**

Southern England
wrap up warm
Northern Ireland
north easterly winds
the East coast of England
the time of year
The cold front moves in over the Atlantic.
Northern Ireland can expect the same.

3 ◀ **T.5.3.A.**

There is a **consonant sound** before and after the sound that disappears and the sound that disappears is itself a consonant sound.

4 **T.5.3.C.**

. . .the west country . . .
. . .the East coast . . .
. . .you can expect some rain . . .
. . .around the three or four degrees mark . . .
. . .the highest spots . . .
. . .the cold front . . .

5 And now here's the weather forecast for the next twenty-four hours for the whole of England, Wales, Scotland and Northern Ireland. Ah starting with Southern England and the Midlands**, well it'll be mainly dry and sunny, but quite cold, with temperatures around six or seven degrees celsius. It should stay dry all day, but there'll be quite a wind, so wrap up warm. And in the west country, Wales and Northern Ireland. You can expect some rain in the morning and afternoon and quite strong north easterly winds**, and the temperature will* be lower than yesterday, around the three or four degrees mark. I don't think you'll see much of the sun:

cloudy all day, I'm afraid. The East coast of England will* see the best of today's weather. It'll be warmer than yesterday, no winds, and sunshine, so quite warm for the time of year. In Scotland and Northern Ireland, however, there'll be heavy rain and maybe some snow during the afternoon, and on the hills temperatures will drop to below freezing, minus four to five, and on the highest spots minus ten. Over much of Scotland it will* be cloudy, and windy too as the cold front moves in over the Atlantic. Northern Ireland can expect the same, but the rain will* end before dark. But again very cold, with temperatures not going above freezing. And that's all from me.

* In fast speech *will* is normally contracted to *'ll*.
** In these words a letter often disappears in the middle of the word because there are three consonants together.

## 4

4 **T.5.4.C.**

a. A I'm going to the supermarket – do you want anything?
   . . .
   B Yes, could you get some biscuits . . . some mayonnaise . . . and some margarine.

b. A I'm going to the greengrocer's – do you want anything?
   . . .
   B Yes, could you get some oranges . . . some bananas . . . and some apples.

c. A I'm going to the newsagent's – do you want anything?
   . . .
   B Yes, could you get some cigarettes . . . some chocolate . . . and some matches.

d. A I'm going to the snack bar – do you want anything?
   . . .
   B Yes, could you get a sandwich . . . a hamburger . . . and some coke.

e. A I'm going to the off licence – do you want anything?
   . . .
   B Yes, could you get some whisky . . . some champagne and some mineral water.

## 5

2 **T.5.5.**

**Sally** I'm going to meet Ann, grandfather.

**Grandfather** You're going to meet Sam? Who's Sam?

**Sally** Not Sam – Ann. We're going to play tennis.

**Grandfather** You're going to play with Dennis? And who's Dennis?

**Sally** Not Dennis. Tennis. We're going to play tennis in the park.

**Grandfather** You're going to play with Dennis and Mark? Who are all these boys you're going to meet?

**Sally** I'm not going to meet any boys, grandfather, I'm going to play tennis in the park – with Ann, a girl . . . oh, never mind . . . see you later!

**Grandfather** Sam . . .? Dennis . . .? Mark . . .? The girl's going mad!

These words are all stressed to give them special emphasis for some reason:

a. Because the speaker is surprised (for example when grandfather says *Sam* or *Dennis*)
b. Because the speaker wants to correct what the other person is saying (for example when Sally says *Not Sam, Ann.*)
c. Because the speaker is impatient (for example when Sally says *I'm not going to meet any boys.*)

## 6

1 **T.5.6.**

1. party          6. America
2. baby           7. violinist
3. divorce        8. jokes
4. birthday       9. election
   presents          results
5. homework      10. film

2 a. disappointed    f. excited
  b. worried         g. interested
  c. shocked         h. amusing
  d. pleased         i. disappointing
  e. annoyed         j. boring

a. We invited thirty people to the party and only six came – we were so *disappointed*.
b. The baby isn't eating enough – I'm a bit *worried* about her.
c. I was so *shocked* when I heard that the Smiths are getting a divorce – they've been married for 25 years!
d. Were you *pleased* with your birthday presents?

95

e. I'm very *annoyed* that none of you have done your homework.

f. I'm going to America next week – I'm terribly *excited* . . . it's the first time I've been.

g. My father's a violinist, but I'm not *interested* in music at all, myself.

h. Jenny can be so *amusing* . . . she's so good at telling jokes!

i. The election results were very *disappointing* for the socialist party – they only got 25% of the vote.

j. That film last night was terribly *boring* – in fact nothing happened at all!

# UNIT 6

## 1

1 `T.6.1.A.`

a. What a wonderful *mill*!
b. Those are high *heels*!
c. Can you *feel* it?
d. This *pitch* is O.K.
e. Don't *slip* now!
f. They lost the *will*.

4 `T.6.1.C.`

|  | /iː/ |  | /ɪ//ɪ/ |
|---|---|---|---|
| a. | cl<u>ea</u>n | h. | l<u>i</u>v<u>i</u>ng room |
|  | /ɪ/ |  | /ɪ//ɪ/ |
| b. | d<u>e</u>tached | i. | m<u>i</u>n<u>u</u>tes |
|  | /iː/ |  | /iː/ |
| c. | conv<u>e</u>nient | j. | p<u>ea</u>ce |
|  | /ɪ/ |  | /ɪ/ |
| d. | cott<u>a</u>ge | k. | r<u>e</u>ception room |
|  | /ɪ/ /ɪ/ |  | /ɪ/ |
| e. | d<u>e</u>scr<u>i</u>ption | l. | r<u>e</u>sidential |
|  | /iː/ |  | /iː/ |
| f. | dr<u>ea</u>m |  | str<u>ee</u>t |
|  | /ɪ/ /ɪ/ |  |  |
| g. | k<u>i</u>tch<u>e</u>n |  |  |

## 2

1 `T.6.2.A.`

*-er* is pronounced / ə /; *-est* is pronounced / ɪst /.

4 `T.6.2.B.`

a. A Which building's the oldest – the Taj Mahal, the Parthenon or the Colosseum?
. . .
B That's right, *the Parthenon's* the oldest.

b. A Which city is the biggest – London, Tokyo or Mexico City?
. . .
B That's right, *Mexico City's* the biggest.

c. A Which country is the smallest – Monaco, Luxemburg or Hungary?
. . .
B That's right, *Monaco's* the smallest.

d. A Which animal is the fastest – the lion, the cheetah or the tiger?
. . .
B That's right *the cheetah's* the fastest.

e. A Which lake's the deepest – Loch Ness, Lake Michigan or Lake Baikal?
. . .
B That's right, *Lake Baikal's* the deepest.

f. A Which bridge is the newest – Tower Bridge, The Golden Gate Bridge or the Bridge of Sighs?
. . .
B That's right. The *Golden Gate Bridge* is the newest.

g. A Which monument's the tallest – the Eiffel Tower, the Statue of Liberty or Nelson's Column?
. . .
B That's right, the *Eiffel Tower's* the tallest.

h. A Which river's the longest – the Mississippi, the Nile or the Danube?
. . .
B That's right, *the Nile's* the longest.

i. A Which mountain's the highest – Mont Blanc, Mount Fuji or Mount Everest?
. . .
B That's right, *Mount Everest's* the highest.

j. A Which planet's the largest – Mars, Jupiter or Venus?
. . .
B That's right, *Jupiter's* the largest.

## 3

1 `T.6.3.A.`

a. Are you *sure*?
b. Take a *ship*.
c. That *seat's* dirty!
d. He *shaved* his master.
e. *Suit* yourself then!

## 4

1

| / s / | / z / |
|---|---|
| press | doesn't |
| us | gloves |
| practise | pounds |
| start | clothes |

| / s / and / z / | / ʃ / |
|---|---|
| slippers | shall |
| sausages | pension |
| pencils | shocked |
| surprised |  |

## 5

1 `T.6.5.`

She's as pretty *as a picture*.
He's as poor as *a church mouse*.
He's as proud as *a peacock*.
She's as deaf as *a post*.
It's as light as *a feather*.
She's as blind as *a bat*.

The adjective and the noun are stressed because they give the message of the sentence.

*as* is pronounced / əz /.

2 He's as poor as a church mouse.

He's as proud as a peacock.

She's as deaf as a post.

It's as light as a feather.

She's as blind as a bat.

## 6

T.6.6.

a. *　　f. **
b. **　　g. **
c. ***　　h. ***
d. ***　　i. *
e. *

## 7

1　T.6.7.A.

No, different words are stressed in each case:

a. fat　b. red-haired　c. fifties.

This word is stressed so strongly, because **B** is correcting a mistake made by **A** over this particular detail of the description.

3　T.6.7.B.

a. 3　d. 2
b. 2　e. 3
c. 1　f. 1

a. Has he got short, dark, curly hair?
b. Was Helen the one in her early thirties?
c. Is it an old red-brick house?
d. Is he mad about watching football?
e. Is he young, rich and intelligent?
f. Has she got a headache, a sore throat, and a temperature?

## 8

1,2　T.6.8.

a. adorable　g. sensitive

b. cheerful　h. sociable

c. inquisitive　i. spontaneous

d. punctual　j. tactful

e. reliable　k. tolerant

f. selfish　l. witty

## 9

3　T.6.9.B.

a. 'You pig, Mary!' Jane said angrily.
b. John, my brother who lives in Oxford, loves fishing.
c. He left his students' English homework in a taxi.
d. 'Is your birthday in February, April?' asked David.

---

# UNIT 7

## 1

1　T.7.1.A.

a. ran　　run
b. sang　　sung
c. rang　　rung
d. swam　　swum
e. began　　begun
f. drank　　drunk

3　T.7.1.B.
a. ran
b. sang
c. rung
d. swum
e. begun
f. drank

4　a. have drunk
b. rang
c. has already begun
d. have just swum
e. drank
f. ran

5　T.7.1.C.

a. incorrect　d. correct
b. correct　　e. correct
c. correct　　f. incorrect

## 2

2　T.7.2.B.

a. Helen ̶has cut ̶her own hair again – it's absolutely horrible!
b. Have you heard about Hanna's horrific adventure in Hamburg?
c. Henry's Uncle Herbert ̶has had another heart attack in hospital.
d. Old Hugh hasn't eaten ̶his ham and eggs already, has ̶he?
e. Hazel and Alan ̶have had another unhappy holiday hitch-hiking in Austria and Hungary.

The words that have silent *h*s are words that are in their weak form, for example *has*, *have* (auxiliary verbs); *his*, *her* (possessive pronouns); *he* (pronoun). Without the / h / sound they can be said more quickly, when they come in the middle of a sentence.

4　The seven 'exceptions' are:

hour　vehicle　exhibition
dishonest　heir　ghost　honest

## 3

1　T.7.3.A.

| / fə / | / fər / |
| --- | --- |
| for ten years | for a week or |
| for two minutes | two |
| for five days | for a long time |
| for six months | for a year |
| | for ever |

2　/ fə / is followed by a consonant – / fər / is followed by a vowel. We pronounce the / r / to link it to the next word.

3 **T.7.3.B.**

a. – How long have you known her?

  . . .

  – Oh, I've known her for fourteen years.

b. – How long has she worked here?

  . . .

  – Oh, she's worked here for ages and ages.

c. – How long have you had that car?

  . . .

  – Oh, I've had it for a couple of months.

d. – How long has he been ill?

  . . .

  – Oh, he's been ill for four or five days.

e. – How long have they been married?

  . . .

  – Oh, they've been married for twenty-five years.

f. – How long have your parents gone away for?

  . . .

  – Oh, they've gone away for a fortnight.

g. – How long has she been a student in this school?

  . . .

  – Oh, she's been a student for about two years.

h. – How long have you been in England?

  . . .

  – Oh, I've been in England for the whole summer.

i. – How long has he been in the bathroom?

  . . .

  – Oh, he's been in the bathroom for a few minutes.

# 4

1 **T.7.4.A.**

In each dialogue, the auxiliary verb in A's sentence is **weak** and in B's sentence is **strong**.

The auxiliary verbs are weak when they come in either an **affirmative** or **question** sentence, if the **full verb** is used. (**Negative** auxiliaries do not have weak forms, only contractions.)

The auxiliary verbs are in the **strong form** when they appear **without the main verb**.

In all the weak forms here the vowel sound is / ə /.

3 **T.7.4.B.**

A Have you ever been to Ireland, Pete?

B Yes, loads of times. My parents go over there every year, you see.

A Do they? Why's that then?

B Oh, my dad was born in Dublin.

A Was he really? He doesn't sound Irish at all.

B No . . . well his family left when he was about ten. What about you? Have you ever been over there?

A Well, we were going to Dublin last summer and then there was that long ferry strike . . .

B That's right there was.

A Anyway we were hoping to go this year instead, but hotel prices have gone up so much . . .

B Yes I know they have, it's terrible. I tell you what, shall I give you my cousin's address? Perhaps you can stay with her for a few days.

A Are you sure we can? It seems a bit cheeky . . .

B No . . .

# 5

1 **T.7.5.A.**

**Margaret** You went to Manchester University, didn't you?

**Steve** Yes, that's right.

**Margaret** But you've worked in Canada for the last ten years, haven't you?

**Steve** Yes, I have.

2 Margaret already knows these facts about Steve. She is only asking to check her information.

*haven't you?* is used with the present perfect;
*didn't you?* is used with the past simple.

5 **T.7.5.C.**

a. . . .

  – You studied computer science at university, didn't you?

  – Yes, that's right.

b. . . .

  – You finished your degree in 1977, didn't you?

  – Yes, that's right.

c. . . .

  – You've worked for Banana Computers since then, haven't you?

  – Yes, that's right.

d. . . .

  – You went to Canada in 1979, didn't you?

  – Yes, that's right.

e. . . .

  – You've also worked in Australia, haven't you?

  – Yes, that's right.

f. . . .

  – You met your wife in Australia, didn't you?

  – Yes, that's right.

g. . . .

  – You've been married for five years, haven't you?

  – Yes, that's right.

h. . . .

  – You and your wife have just had a baby, haven't you?

  – Yes, that's right.

# 6

| / ə / | / æ / |
|---|---|
| • | • |
| abroad | Anglo-Tours |
| • | • |
| attend | application |
| • | • |
| applied | actually |
| • | |
| address | |

| / eɪ / | / eə / |
|---|---|
| • | • |
| aged | area |

| / ɑː / |
|---|
| • |
| answer |

2 In the words beginning with / ə / the stress is *never* on the *first* syllable. This is because / ə / is never stressed. The stress is usually on the **second** syllable in these words.

In other words the stress is usually on the **first** syllable.

3 ⌈ **T.7.6.** ⌉

| / ə / | / æ / |
|---|---|
| America | accent |
| around | Africa |
| Atlantic | |
| attractive | |
| about | |
| amusing | |
| ago | |
| arrive | |
| agree | |
| alone | |

| / eɪ / | / eə / |
|---|---|
| Asia | aeroplane |
| able | |

| / ɑː / |
|---|
| — |

## 7

2 ⌈ **T.7.7.A.** ⌉

a. England and Scotland have had the same king since *1603*.
b. Britain hasn't governed the United States since *1776*.
c. Women in Britain have had the vote since *1919*.
d. Elizabeth II has been Queen since *1952*.
e. England hasn't been successfully invaded since *1066*.

f. Britain hasn't governed India since *1947*.
g. Britain has been a member of the European Community since *1973*.
h. Britain hasn't had a successful revolution since *1649*.

## 8

2 ⌈ **T.7.8.** ⌉

TA Hello, Pentagon Travel.
C Hello, I'd like to fly return to Madrid. Can you tell me how much it would cost?
TA When would you like to travel?
C I'd like to go on Sunday, the *twenty-third of September* and come back on Friday, the *twenty-eighth of September*.
TA Well . . . I'm afraid you'll have to pay the full fare then . . . that's . . . *£369* return.
C As much as that!
TA You can't wait and come back on the thirtieth?
C Does that make a difference?
TA Yes, you can get a special reduction if you stay for seven days – it would only be *£179*.
C Oh, that's quite a big difference, isn't it? I'll do that then. Can you give me the times and the flight numbers?
TA Yes, on the way there you leave London Heathrow at *9.55* and arrive in Madrid at *11.45*. The flight number's *BA 741*.
C And coming back?
TA You come back in the afternoon – you leave Madrid at 16.20 – that's *twenty past four* and arrive back at Heathrow at 18.10 – that's *ten past six*. Shall I make a reservation then, Madam?
C Yes, please. My name's Susan Sarrell – that's *S–A–R–R–E–L–L*.
TA Thank you. And could I

have your address and telephone number too, please?
C Yes it's ten *Rookery* Avenue . . .
TA How do you spell that?
C *R–O–O–K–E–R–Y*. It's London *SE13*. The phone number's *983–2115*.
TA Right, thanks a lot. Remember, you should pay before the fifteenth of September.
C Fine . . . thank you for your help. Goodbye.
TA Goodbye.

## UNIT 8

### 1

1
| | |
|---|---|
| a. ti<u>r</u>ed | d. b<u>ur</u>y |
| b. w<u>or</u>n | e. w<u>ea</u>r |
| c. w<u>es</u>tern | |

3 ⌈ **T.8.1.B.** ⌉

A Are all your friends from univ<u>er</u>sity w<u>or</u>king now?
B Nearly. K<u>ir</u>sty's doing res<u>ear</u>ch w<u>or</u>k at B<u>ir</u>mingham univ<u>er</u>sity and Shirley's gone to w<u>or</u>k as a n<u>ur</u>se in the Th<u>ir</u>d World – B<u>ur</u>ma or somewhere.
A Really? That's adventurous. What about P<u>ear</u>l?
B Oh, P<u>ear</u>l's t<u>ur</u>ned really cons<u>er</u>vative. She's a civil s<u>er</u>vant now. She and K<u>ir</u>k live in some sub<u>ur</u>b somewhere.
A And how about D<u>ir</u>k?
B Oh, haven't you h<u>ear</u>d about D<u>ir</u>k? He's w<u>or</u>king in T<u>ur</u>key as a winds<u>ur</u>f instructor! He's l<u>ear</u>nt T<u>ur</u>kish and he's <u>ear</u>ning a fortune, or so I've h<u>ear</u>d.

### 2

1 ⌈ **T.8.2.A.** ⌉

| /m/ | /m/ |
|---|---|
| Green Park | London Bridge |
| /g/ | /m/ |
| Wood Green | Boston Manor |

/m(p)/ /k/
Holland Park    Brent Cross
/m(p)/ /p/
Saint Paul's    Great Portland
                Street
/k/
High Street
Kensington

3   T.8.2.B.

Marble Arch      East Putney

West Brompton    North Ealing

Mile End         Bond Street

Old Street       West Acton

## 3

1   T.8.3.

a. 8    d. 6    g. 8
b. 8    e. 7    h. 7
c. 7    f. 8    i. 7

a. I *think we should* tell *him about* it.
b. *I haven't got to do it today*.
c. *You don't have to* tell me.
d. *He has to* work *very* hard.
e. *Do you have to go home already?*
f. *I've got to* be *there at* nine.
g. *We really* mustn't *be late, you know*.
h. *What do you* think I *should do?*
i. I *don't think you should* worry.

2   The *t* in *mustn't* is **not** heard.
    *Should* is **not** stressed. If it is
    stressed it sounds very emphatic
    and in the wrong situation it
    could sound rude.
    The sound / v / in *have* changes
    to / f / (/ hæftə /). The sound
    / z / in *has* changes to / s /
    (/ hæstə /).

## 4

1   T.8.4.A.

You should *hold your breath*.
You should *drink a glass of water*.
You should *take a little lemon juice*.

3   T.8.4.C.

a. A  I've got a terrible cold!
       . . .
   B  You should go to bed.
b. A  Trains in Britain are so
       expensive!
       . . .
   B  You should take the bus.
c. A  My hands are freezing
       cold!
       . . .
   B  You should wear gloves.
d. A  I feel so sleepy!
       . . .
   B  You should have a cup of
       coffee.
e. A  I've got the most terrible
       toothache!
       . . .
   B  You should go to the
       dentist's.
f. A  I feel so unfit these days!
       . . .
   B  You should start jogging.
g. A  I never practise speaking
       English!
       . . .
   B  You should go to England.
h. A  I've got an awful cough
       again!
       . . .
   B  You should stop smoking.

## 5

1   why        some
    good       exercise
    idea       vigorously
    doctor     soon
    starting   result
    think      injuries
    not        long
    fit        heal

2   Generally the words in the
    sentence which carry the
    message are stressed (nouns,
    verbs and adjectives). The words
    which are not stressed are
    auxiliary verbs, pronouns,
    possessive adjectives (*his*, *her*
    etc.), prepositions and articles
    (*a*, *the*).

Many of these words become
weak forms. Here the weak
forms would be: *can* / kən /, *be*
/ bɪ /, *are* / ər / or / ə /, *a* / ə /, *to*
/ tə / or / tʊ /, *your* / jə /, *you*
jə / or / jʊ /, *some* / səm /, *and*
/ ənd /, *as* / əz /.

## 6

1   young – *youth*
    energetic – *energy*
    strong – *strength*
    beautiful – *beauty*
    old – *age*

3   Some adjectives ending in -*less*
    (there are many more):

    colourless    fearless
    endless       homeless
    fatherless    meaningless
    faultless     motherless
    powerless     shapeless
    penniless     thoughtless

## 7

2   • treatment / 'tri:tmənt /

    • poison / 'pɔɪzən /

    breathe / bri:ð /

    breath / breθ /

    • injury / 'ɪndʒərɪ /

    • muscle / 'mʌsl̩ /

    • aching / 'eɪkɪŋ /

    health / helθ /

    heal / hi:l /

    heart / hɑ:t /

    sprained / spreɪnd /

    • swollen / 'swəʊlən /

    sore / sɔ: /

    bruise / bru:z /

    • bandage / 'bændɪdʒ /

# 9

**1** | T.8.9.A. |

| | |
|---|---|
| half | point one |
| a quarter | point five |
| a fifth | point seven five |
| two-thirds | point two eight five |
| five-twelfths | point nought seven |

**2** | T.8.9.B. |

a. What's another way of saying 'half'?

. . .

.5

b. What's another way of saying 'a fifth'?

. . .

.2

c. What's another way of saying 'a tenth'?

. . .

.1

d. What's another way of saying 'a quarter'?

. . .

.25

e. What's another way of saying 'an eighth'?

. . .

.125

f. What's another way of saying 'a hundredth'?

. . .

.01

g. What's another way of saying '.6'?

. . .

three-fifths

h. What's another way of saying '.03'?

. . .

three hundredths

i. What's another way of saying '.05'?

. . .

a twentieth.

**5** a. iii   e. i
b. ii   f. iii
c. ii   g. ii
d. i   h. ii

---

# UNIT 9

## 1

**2** | T.9.1.B. |

a. Have a *sherry*.
b. I cut my *shin* badly.
c. I love *ships*.
d. What a big *chop*!
e. What's in that *ditch*?
f. Can you *watch* the window?

**5** | T.9.1.D. |

a. Which of Shirley Hatchard's children stole a portion of cherry cheesecake from the kitchen shelf?
b. Sheila Charlton's Czech washing machine chewed up Richard Sheridan's checked shorts.
c. The rich Turkish sugar merchant purchased a shining Porsche for his Chinese chauffeur to polish.
d. Sasha, the Russian chess champion, chased Sharon, the Scottish chambermaid round the kitchen floor, so Sharon showed Sasha the door.

## 2

**1** | T.9.2.A. |

a. 1   e. 1
b. 2   f. 1
c. 2   g. 2
d. 2   h. 1

**2** a. 'll help . . . want
b. 'd go . . . was
c. 'd work . . . paid
d. 'd be . . . told
e. 'll stay . . . is
f. is . . . 'll phone
g. 'd come . . . had
h. isn't . . . 'll lose

---

# 3

**1** | T.9.3.A. |

a. A   f. A
b. U   g. U
c. A   h. U
d. A   i. A
e. U

**3** | T.9.3.B. |

a. J   If I lived in a city, I'd prefer to live in the centre rather than the suburbs, wouldn't you?

. . .

b. J   I'd like to live near the shops and the main road, wouldn't you?

. . .

c. J   If I could, I'd love to live high up, on the top floor, wouldn't you?

. . .

d. J   If I could afford it, I'd love to have my own sauna, wouldn't you?

. . .

e. M   If I could choose, I'd prefer to live in a small village in the country, wouldn't you?

. . .

f. M   I'd like to have a really big garden with lots of flowers and trees, wouldn't you?

. . .

g. M   And I'd love to have lots of pets, wouldn't you?

. . .

h. M   If I could afford it, I would most like to have my own swimming pool, wouldn't you?

. . .

## 4

**1** T.9.4.

| 1. ● | 2. ● ● |
|------|--------|
| bedroom | French windows |
| dining-room | double glazing |
| living-room | central heating |
| fireplace | fitted wardrobes |
| utility room | fitted carpets |
| loft space | |
| air conditioning | |

**2** With **noun/gerund** + **noun** there is only **one** stress.
With **adjective** + **noun** there are **two** stresses.

## 5

**1** T.9.5.

*-ture* is pronounced / t ʃə /.
The exception is *mature*, where the ending is pronounced / t jʊə /. Here the ending is stressed; in the other words the ending is not stressed.

.3
  ● agricultural

  ● architectural

● cultural

● natural

  ● structural

## 6

**1** × multiply (by)
− subtract (from)
+ add (and)
÷ divide (by)

**3** T.9.6.A.

a. If you *add* 2 *and* 5, you get 7.
b. If you *multiply* 3.5 *by* 2, you get 7.
c. If you *subtract* 6 *from* 13, you get 7.
d. If you *divide* 28 *by* 4, you get 7.

**3** T.9.6.B.

You always finish with the number 7.

a. Write down any number between 1 and 10.
b. If you add 2 to your number, what do you get?
c. Now multiply that number by 2, what do you get?
d. Add ten to the number, what do you get?
e. Now multiply this number by 0.5, what do you get?
f. Subtract the first number that you thought of, what do you get?

## 7

**1** T.9.7.A.

centimetre . . . inch
metre . . . yard
square metre . . . acre
kilometre . . . mile
litre . . . pint
gram . . . ounce
kilogram . . . pound

*Stone* would be measured in *kilos*;
*Gallons* would be measured in *litres*;
*Feet* would be measured in *centimetres*.

**2** T.9.7.B.

a. One inch equals 2.54 centimetres.
b. One foot equals 30.48 centimetres.
c. One yard equals .91 metres.
d. One acre equals 4,446.86 square metres.
e. One mile equals 1.61 kilometres.
f. One pint equals .57 litres.
g. One gallon equals 4.55 litres.
h. One ounce equals 28.53 grams.
i. One pound equals .454 kilos.
j. One stone equals 6.35 kilos.

**3** T.9.7.C.

| Place |
|-------|
| a. greengrocer's/supermarket |
| b. grocer's/corner shop |
| c. pub/restaurant |
| d. sweet shop |
| e. grocer's/corner shop |
| f. material shop/department store |
| g. petrol station |
| h. butcher's/supermarket |

| Quantity |
|----------|
| a. a pound |
| b. half a pound |
| c. half a pint |
| d. four ounces |
| e. two pints |
| f. two and a half yards |
| g. six gallons |
| h. eight ounces |

| Goods |
|-------|
| a. grapes |
| b. butter |
| c. lager |
| d. chocolate drops |
| e. milk |
| f. striped material |
| g. four star petrol |
| h. minced beef |

a. A Yes please?
  B Could I have a pound of grapes, please?
b. A I'll have half a pound of butter, please . . .
  B Is that everything?

c.  A  Half a pint of lager, please.
    B  Half a pint of lager . . .
       anything else?
d.  A  Yes love . . .?
    B  I'd like four ounces of
       chocolate drops, please.
e.  A  Can I have two pints of
       milk, please?
    B  Sorry love, we've run out.
f.  A  Can I help you madam?
    B  I'd like 2½ yards of that
       striped material, please.
g.  A  Yes madam.
    B  I'll have 6 gallons of the
       four star, please.
h.  A  Can I have 8 ounces of
       minced beef, please?
    B  Certainly sir.

# UNIT 10

## 1

1
| /e/ | /eɪ/ |
| --- | --- |
| dreamt | paid |
| read | waited |
| said | lay |
| ate | failed |
| meant | laid |
|  | made |
|  | ate |

3
| /e/ | /eɪ/ |
| --- | --- |
| felt | stayed |
| met | hated |
| lent | played |
| left |  |
| slept |  |

## 2

2  Rules for when *r* is pronounced
   and when it is not:
   a. *r* is pronounced when it
      comes before the vowel
      sound in the syllable.
   b. *r* is **not** pronounced when it
      comes after the vowel sound
      in the syllable.

c.  If it comes at the end of the
    word (or syllable) *r* is
    pronounced if the next word
    or syllable begins with a
    vowel.

## 3

1  Can . . . can . . . can't . . .
   can . . . can . . . can't . . .
   can . . . can't . . . can . . .
   can't . . .

2  *Can* is unstressed. It is
   pronounced / kən / when it is
   weak.

   *Can't* is stressed. It is
   pronounced / kɑːnt /.

## 4

1    T.10.4.

   A  How long are you here *for*?
   B  Only *for* another couple *of*
      days.
   C  My brother's working *at*
      MacDonald's this summer!
   D  Oh, what's he working *as*?
   C  *As* a cook!
   E  Where's the other half *of* that
      bottle *of* whisky?
   F  You left it *at* the bottom *of*
      the stairs.
   G  Would you like *to* come back
      *to* my flat *for* a drink?
   H  I'd love *to*.

2  The **weak forms** are *at* /ət /; *as*
   / əz /; *to* / tə / or / tʊ /; *for*
   / fə / or / fər /; *from*
   / frəm /, and *of* / əv /.

   The **strong forms** are *at* / æt /; *as*
   / æz /; *to* / tuː /; *for* / fɔː /;
   *from* / frɒm /, and *of* / ɒv /.

   | A S | E W |
   | --- | --- |
   | B W | F W |
   | C W | G W |
   | D S | H S |
   | C W | |

   In these dialogues the strong
   forms are used when the words
   come at the end of the sentence
   or question.

## 5

1    T.10.5.A.

didn't they?

won't he?

2  Complete the rule:
   a. down
   b. up

3    T.10.5.B.

   a. ↗   c. ↘   e. ↘   g. ↘
   b. ↗   d. ↘   f. ↗   h. ↗

## 6

1    T.10.6.A.

   1. Could I borrow this record?
   c. Well, actually . . . it's not
      mine.
   2. Do you mind if I turn off the
      fire?
   g. Well, actually . . . I'm a bit
      cold.
   3. Could you possibly give me a
      lift to the station?
   d. Well, actually . . . there's
      something wrong with the
      car.
   4. Do you think I could borrow
      your jeans?
   e. Well, actually . . . they're
      dirty at the moment.
   5. Do you mind if I turn up the
      music?
   h. Well, actually . . . my
      flatmate's gone to bed.
   6. Could you possibly lend me
      £5?
   b. Well, actually . . . I've only
      got £5 myself.
   7. Would you mind typing this
      letter for me, before you go
      home?
   f. Well, actually . . . I'm in a bit
      of a hurry.
   8. Do you mind if I smoke?
   a. Well, actually . . . we don't
      like smoking.

## 7

1 | **T.10.7.A.**

a. **W** This kitchen floor's absolutely filthy!
   **M** Well let's clean it then.

b. **M** What did your boss say when you told him you were leaving?
   **W** Oh, he was absolutely furious!

c. **W** Your neighbours have got a big dog, haven't they?
   **M** They certainly have . . . it's absolutely terrifying!

d. **W** I think all this violence on TV is absolutely disgusting!
   **M** Well write to the BBC and tell them!

e. **W** This fish soup's absolutely delicious! How did you make it?
   **M** It's out of a tin actually.

f. **M** What's the heating like in your new flat?
   **W** Not very good – the bedroom's absolutely freezing.

g. **W** Why have you left all the car windows open?
   **M** Oh, it was absolutely boiling inside!

h. **M** Cynthia knows an awful lot about politics, doesn't she?
   **W** Yes . . . some of her theories are absolutely fascinating!

i. **W** Have you been to that new hypermarket yet?
   **M** Yes, it's absolutely vast!

j. **W** How was it moving house?
   **M** Absolutely exhausting!

k. **W** Have you seen the new Woody Allen film yet?
   **M** Mmm. It was absolutely hilarious!

l. **W** Doesn't that book have rather a strange ending?
   **M** Yes, it's absolutely astonishing! You don't expect it at all!

## 8

2 | **T.10.8.A.**

| 1 ● ● | 2 ● ● ● |
|---|---|
| music | chemistry |
| physics | algebra |
| science | politics |
| history | literature |

| 3 ● ● ● | 4 ● ● ● ● |
|---|---|
| statistics | philosophy |
| computing | psychology |
| mathematics | biology |
| | geology |
| | geometry |
| | geography |

| 5 ● ● ● ● | 6 ● ● ● ● ● |
|---|---|
| economics | sociology |
| engineering | archaeology |

3   a. literature
    b. mathematics (or algebra)
    c. economics
    d. history
    e. philosophy
    f. archaeology
    g. biology
    h. psychology

| **T.10.8.B.**

a. The thing I enjoyed most last term was Shakespeare's love sonnets.

b. It was the one subject I really hated at school. I mean, I'm just hopeless with numbers of any kind.

c. At the moment we're studying inflation and its effect on interest rates – it's quite interesting.

d. Personally, I'm more interested in the modern stuff – from after the French Revolution, let's say.

e. The most important thing is logical thinking – I mean, yes, you learn about Plato or Descartes or whoever . . . but I don't think that's the most important thing.

f. I like it most when we're out digging. Last summer for example, we went to a Roman site in the south of France.

g. People think we spend all our time cutting up dead animals, but we don't, of course!

h. In the first term of the course you study the history of the subject, you know Freud and Jung and that sort of thing, but after that it's more practical.

## 9

1 | **T.10.9.**

a. **A** There was a strike where I work that lasted ten months.
   . . .
   **B** What? A ten-month strike!

b. **A** That woman over there's got a daughter who's twenty-three years old!
   . . .
   **B** What? A twenty-three-year-old daughter!

c. **A** And she's got another daughter – a baby who's only six months old!
   . . .
   **B** What? A six-month-old baby!

d. **A** The Turners are going to Jamaica on holiday for seven weeks.
   . . .
   **B** What? A seven-week holiday!

e. **A** My sister and her husband live in a cottage which is five hundred years old.
   . . .
   **B** What? A five-hundred-year-old cottage!

f. **A** I've got a present for you – a kitten! It's only three weeks old!
   . . .
   **B** What? A three-week-old kitten?

g. **A** Across the road from my house there's a

supermarket that's open
twenty-four hours a day.
. . .

  B What? A twenty-four-hour
supermarket!

h. A Last weekend I played
tennis with my granny
who's seventy-five years
old.
. . .

  B What? With your seventy-
five-year-old granny!

# UNIT 11

## 1

1 | T.11.1.A. |

a. Do you want a *vet*?
b. I only want the *best*!
c. Shall we take a *vote*?
d. I think there's something
wrong with my *vowels*.
e. There are some *bats* in the
cellar.

## 2

2 | T.11.2.B. |

a. There's some *cork* in the
bottle.
b. That's a nice red plastic *bowl*.
c. It isn't far to the *show* from
here.
d. How many *noughts* can you
see?
e. Let me *saw* it for you.

## 3

1 Margaret  Robert  John
Susan  William  Andrew
Catherine  Thomas
Charles  Elizabeth

2 | T.11.3.A. |

Maggie and Susie
Bobby and Billy
Johnny and Andy
Cathy and Charlie
Tommy and Lizzie

3 All these names end with the
sound / ə /. They are therefore
linked together with an extra
/ r / sound, *Linda and
Hannah* etc.

| T.11.3.B. |

Linda and Hannah
Sarah and Sheila*
Sandra and Amanda*
Laura and Patricia*

* With these names which
already contain / r / the final
/ ə / is elided and the / r / and
the linking / r / merge when
speaking at speed, e.g.
/ seərəndʃi: lə /
/ lɔ: rənpətrɪʃə /.

4 They are linked together with an
extra / w / sound. (This is
because the word before *and*
ends with a vowel made at the
*back* of the mouth.)
*Romeo* /w/ *and Juliet*

5 | T.11.3.D. |

Kennedy /j/ and Kruschev

Plato /w/ and Aristotle

Franco /w/ and Mussolini

Victoria /r/ and Albert

Isabella /r/ and Ferdinand

Diana /r/ and Charles

Mary /j/ and Joseph

Yoko Ono /w/ and John Lennon

Antony /j/ and Cleopatra

Mickey /j/ and Minnie Mouse

6 | T.11.3.E. |

a. My aeroplane arrives in
/j/
Australia at about eight
/r/
o'clock in the evening.
/j/
b. Uncle Alfie and Auntie Elsie
/j/
always go away at Easter.
/w/  /j/

c. Are you asking us to accept
/w/    /w/
an offer of only eighty
/j/
pounds?

d. Nicky and Laura are off to
/j/    /r/    /w/
Italy and Austria again.
/j/    /r/

e. Bruno and Anna are arriving
/w/    /r/
in an hour or so and they're
/w/
often early.

## 4

1 a. Well, no actually, I've been
■
driving for two years.

b. Well, no actually, I've been
■
studying English for six
months.

c. Well, no actually, I've been
collecting coins since I left
■
school.

d. Well, no actually, I've been
■
playing the guitar since 1980.

e. Well, no actually, I've been
■
painting the outside of the
house since Monday.

f. Well, no actually, I've been
■
singing in operas since I was
eighteen.

2 These words are stressed
because they are the most
important for correcting the
mistakes that **A** has made.

**3** **T.11.4.B.**

a. **A** So you've been living in the United States since you left school.

   . . .

   **B** Well, no actually, I've been living in *Canada* since I left school.

b. **A** So you've been using this book for a few days . . .

   . . .

   **B** Well, no actually, I've been using this book for a few *months*.

c. **A** So you've been waiting for two hours . . .

   . . .

   **B** Well, no actually, I've been waiting for *four* hours.

d. **A** So you've been teaching English for several years . . .

   . . .

   **B** Well, no actually, I've been *learning* English for several years.

e. **A** You've been playing squash this morning, haven't you?

   . . .

   **B** Well, no actually, I've been playing *tennis* this morning.

f. **A** You've just been reading a newspaper article, haven't you?

   . . .

   **B** Well, no actually, I've just been *writing* a newspaper article.

g. **A** You've been cooking fish, haven't you?

   . . .

   **B** Well, no actually, I've been cooking *meat*.

h. **A** John's been jogging, hasn't he?

   . . .

   **B** Well, no actually, he's been *cycling*.

i. **A** You've been working here since nineteen eighty-one, haven't you?

   . . .

   **B** Well, no actually, I've

been working here since nineteen *seventy-one*.

j. **A** You've been washing all morning, haven't you?

   . . .

   **B** Well, no actually, I've been *ironing* all morning.

**5**

**1** **T.11.5.A.**

a. *long*      e. *tall*
b. *many*      f. *far*
c. *often*     g. *thick*
d. *old*       h. *much*

**4** **T.11.5.C.**

a. **A** One of my colleagues lives in a caravan in the middle of the country.

   . . .

   **B** Where does he live?

b. **A** He lives there with his elderly aunt.

   . . .

   **B** Who does he live with?

c. **A** He's also got nine dogs there with him.

   . . .

   **B** How many dogs has he got?

d. **A** He lives ten miles away from the nearest village.

   . . .

   **B** How far away does he live?

e. **A** He travels everywhere in a vintage Rolls Royce.

   . . .

   **B** How does he travel?

f. **A** He always wears shorts and sandals, even in winter.

   . . .

   **B** What does he wear?

g. **A** In his spare time he plays the trumpet.

   . . .

   **B** What does he play?

h. **A** And as a hobby, he collects animals' teeth.

   . . .

   **B** What does he collect?

**6**

**2** **T.11.6.A.**

a. a profitable business

b. an unreliable car

c. an understandable mistake

d. a readable book

e. a dependable chap

f. an unforgettable evening

g. unacceptable behaviour

h. an unbelievable story

i. an unavoidable situation

j. an unbreakable rule

k. a likeable person

l. an uncontrollable madman

**3** **T.11.6.B.**

a. understandably
b. enjoyably
c. unreasonably
d. unprofitably
e. unbelievably
f. capably
g. unacceptably
h. unforgivably

**7**

**1**  a. brush        g. cabinet
    b. card         h. lamp
    c. machine      i. boots
    d. board        j. pin
    e. book         k. pot
    f. paper        l. case

The first word carries the main stress in each case.

**2** **T.11.7.**

a. paintbrush
   toothbrush
   clothes brush
   hairbrush

b. birthday card
Christmas card
Valentine card
get well card

c. washing machine
coffee machine
sewing machine
answering machine

d. blackboard
noticeboard
chessboard
scoreboard

e. cheque book
recipe book
address book
telephone book

f. wrapping paper
writing paper
notepaper      t
wallpaper

g. drinks cabinet
filing cabinet
medicine cabinet
china cabinet

h. table lamp
desk lamp
wall lamp        ;
reading lamp

i. climbing boots
football boots
wellington boots
riding boots

j. rolling pin
drawing pin
hairpin
safety pin

k. flowerpot
coffee pot
pepperpot
teapot

l. bookcase
suitcase
pencil case
briefcase

## 8

1   T.11.8.A.

*NASA*, *NATO* and *OPEC* are always said as words. *UFO* and *VAT* are usually spelt out, but can be said as words.

3   a. RAF      d. CND
b. IRA      e. VAT
c. VIP      f. OPEC

---

g. AIDS      i. BC
h. DIY       j. EEC

---

# UNIT 12

## 1

a. 2      d. 1
b. 1      e. 1
c. 1      f. 2

1,2   T.12.1.A.

a. thin . . . thing
b. fang . . . fan
c. wing . . . win
d. rang . . . ran
e. sung . . . sun
f. ban . . . bang

3   / g / *is* pronounced in the following words:

finger      Hungary
longer      tango
mango       hunger
single      strongest

(Generally it is *not* pronounced when what follows is a **suffix**, rather than an integral part of the word – the **exception** is comparatives and superlatives.)

## 2

1   T.12.2.A.

a. four      d. route
b. lower     e. grown
c. show

4   T.12.2.B.

a. I found £50 lying on the ground when I was in town this morning.
b. Laura's going to show you round the house now.
c. We caught a little brown mouse in the shower room downstairs this morning.
d. They've got a town house *and* a country house you know.
e. They lowered the cow to the ground from the window of the tower.

---

## 3

1   T.12.3.

a. 8      c. 10      e. 7
b. 9      d. 11      f. 14

a. *Are you* doing *anything special on* Thursday *night*?
b. *We're having a* party *at the* weekend, *okay*?
c. *Are you* going *out* tonight, *or are you* staying *in*?
d. *Sorry, but the* manager *isn't coming back* until *after* lunch.
e. *Are you seeing* Dave *again* tomorrow *night*?
f. *We're meeting in* front *of the* theatre *tomorrow* night at half past seven.

The stressed words are the content words (**nouns, main verbs** and **adjectives**, usually).

The weak forms are generally **prepositions, auxiliary verbs, pronouns, possessive adjectives, articles** and **conjunctions** (*and, but* etc.).

The weak forms here are pronounced:

a. *are* / ə /, *you* / jə /.
b. *a* / ə /, *at* / ət /, *the* / ðə /.
c. *are you* . . . (as above)
d. *but* / bət /; *the* / ðə /.
e. *Are you* . . . (as above)
f. *of* / əv / (*the* and *at* as above)

## 4

2   T.12.4.

**Steve**  Hello this is Steve – can I speak to Alison please?

**Paul**  I'm afraid she's having a shower at the moment – can she ring you back?

**Steve**  Mmm . . . well, all right but I'm going out in a couple of minutes. I'll be back in about two hours okay – can she pho**m**e me back then?

**Paul** I thin**k** she's going out later

herself – oh hang on, she's jus**t**

coming out of the shower – I'll

pa**s** you over to her okay . . .

## 5

2  T.12.5.A.

a. Linda McCartney, the wife of Paul McCartney, lives a quiet life in the country.
b. Mary Padley, a hundred-and-three-year-old London woman, smokes 60 cigarettes a day.
c. Linda Smaje, a thirty-nine-year-old housewife from London, has gone bankrupt because of credit card spending.
d. Olive Gibbs, a seventy-two-year-old woman from Sussex, has travelled the world in a camping van.
e. Nicky Bennett-Rees, a nurse from London, is taking part in a sponsored climb of Mt. Kilimanjaro.
f. Ruth Lawrence, a ten-year-old girl from Huddersfield, has won a scholarship to Oxford.

## 6

1  T.12.6.

a. The manager has *put* the meeting *off* until tomorrow.
b. *Look at* that man in the funny hat!
c. His parents died when he was six, so really his grandmother *brought* him *up*.
d. I'm *looking for* the scissors, I can't find them anywhere.
e. Lynne *came round* for a chat this afternoon.
f. I don't know what's happened to Kevin. We've been *waiting for* him for the

last two hours and he's not usually late.

g. When she hasn't got anyone to play with she often *makes* imaginary friends *up* and then she talks to them for hours!
h. *Listen to* that noise outside!
i. Could you possibly *put* me *up* for the night when I come down to London for my interview?
j. The plane *took off* but had to make an emergency landing again almost immediately.
k. Both of the children *take after* their mother's side of the family. They're not like their father at all.
l. They're going to *pull* the old village church *down*, you know. They say it's a public danger.

2  The following adverbs/prepositions are stressed:

| a. off | e. round | i. up |
| b. — | f. — | j. off |
| c. up | g. up | k. — |
| d. — | h. — | l. down |

## 7

1

● oxygen             ● diameter

● solar energy        ● hydro-electric power

● astronaut           ● nitrogen

● globe               ● rotation

● nuclear power       ● circumference

● axis                plant

● hydrogen            space

● radius

2  T.12.7.

| a | b |
| --- | --- |
| oxygen | diameter |
| nitrogen | circumference |
| hydrogen | radius |

| c | d |
| --- | --- |
| solar energy | globe |
| hydro-electric power | rotation |
| | axis |
| nuclear power | |

| e |
| --- |
| astronaut |
| planet |
| space |

## 8

3  T.12.8.B.

a. Which is the highest mountain range in the world?
. . .
The Himalayas.
b. Which is the deepest ocean in the world?
. . .
The Pacific.
c. Where was Captain Scott trying to go?
. . .
To the South Pole.
d. Which is the longest river in the world?
. . .
The Nile.
e. Which mountain range lies between France and Spain?
. . .
The Pyrenees.
f. Which river goes through London?
. . .
The Thames.
g. Where is the North Pole, in the Arctic or the Antarctic?
. . .
In the Arctic.
h. Which is the longest canal in the world?
. . .
The Panama.
i. Which is the longest river in Europe?
. . .
The Rhine.

# UNIT 13

## 1

1 [T.13.1.A.]

Good food
Cookery Book
A New Look
A book of cartoons
Good Afternoon
push or pull?
The School Rules
Football Pools
News Bulletin
A room with a view

3 The following words do **not** have an extra / j / sound before the / u : / sound:

| | |
|---|---|
| do | fool |
| boots | cool |
| flew | tool |

4 [T.13.1.C.]

     /u:/    /ʊ/ /u:/
a. No news is good news.
    /ʊ/
b. I wouldn't like to be in your
    /u:/
shoes
       /u:/
c. He's getting too big for his
  /u:/
boots.
    /u:/     /ʊ/
d. The proof of the pudding is in the eating.
    /u:/ /ʊ/     /u:/
e. It's too good to be true.
      /u:/ /u:/
f. He's got a screw loose.

## 2

3 [T.13.2.A.]

| | | | | | |
|---|---|---|---|---|---|
| a. P | d. P | g. P |
| b. P | e. P | h. A |
| c. A | f. P | i. A |

a. 173 people have been killed in a plane crash over the Alps.
b. Six men are being questioned at Greenfields Police Station

about the IRA bomb attack last week.
c. The Prince and Princess of Wales have been enjoying a day of sightseeing during their tour of India.
d. Over three thousand new jobs will be created when the new Ford factory opens near Manchester, says the Prime Minister.
e. Several hundred people have been arrested in demonstrations in Warsaw.
f. The building of the new Thames bridge will not be started until next year, it has been announced.
g. In London today a small Picasso drawing has been sold for over three million pounds.
h. Tutu, the giant panda, has returned to London Zoo today after her operation last week.
i. Finally, a seventy-five year old London man has married again – for the ninth time!

3 [T.13.2.B.]

a. (*Sound*) . . .
An American warplane has been shot down over the Mediterranean.
b. (*Sound*) . . .
43 people have been killed in a train crash near Glasgow.
c. (*Sound*) . . .
12 British soccer hooligans were arrested in Paris last night.
d. (*Sound*) . . .
The British company, General Engines, will be sold next month to an American electrical company.
e. (*Sound*) . . .
There has been a General Election in New Zealand today.
f. (*Sound*) . . .
A man is being questioned by London police tonight about the murder of a 7-year-old girl.

g. (*Sound*) . . .
The Queen has been visiting an isolated Amazonian tribe today, during her official visit to Brazil.
h. (*Sound*) . . .
The oldest man in Britain has died in a Birmingham hospital today, aged 113.

## 3

2 [T.13.3.A.]

a. i *very*
a. ii *too*
b. i *very*
b. ii *too*
c. i *very*
c. i *too*
d. i *too*
d. ii *very*

All the adjectives begin with a **vowel sound**. *Too* and *very* also end with a vowel sound – this is why there can be an extra linking sound. Notice that this only happens in **fast** speech.

There is a linking / j / sound after *very* because *very* ends with a **front** vowel. There is a linking / w / sound after *too* because *too* ends with a back vowel.

3 [T.13.3.B.]

There is **no** linking sound with *very dangerous*, *very rude* and *very sad*. There can be linking in all the other cases.

4 [T.13.3.C.]

There can be **no** extra linking / w / sound with *too polite*, *too dishonest* and *too unhappy*. There can be in all the other cases.

## 4

1 T.13.4.A.

a. A    c. A    e. B    g. A
b. B    d. B    f. B    h. B

4 T.13.4.C.

a. **A** We had a *lovely* time!

    . . .

   **B** Well, it was *quite* enjoyable . . .

b. **A** We met some *fascinating* people!

    . . .

   **B** Well, they were *quite* interesting . . .

c. **A** And the people in all the little towns were *so friendly!*

    . . .

   **B** Well, they were *quite* nice . . .

d. **A** The train service in France was really *excellent*!

    . . .

   **B** Well, it was *quite* good . . .

e. **A** And the camp-sites were *such good value* for money!

    . . .

   **B** Well, they were *quite* cheap . . .

f. **A** And it was absolutely *spotless* everywhere!

    . . .

   **B** Well, it was *quite* clean . . .

g. **A** And of course, everywhere we went the food was *so delicious!*

    . . .

   **B** Well, it was *quite* good . . .

h. **A** And as for the weather – it was *boiling* every day!

    . . .

   **B** Well, it was *quite* hot . . .

i. **A** Underneath all these clothes we're really *tanned*!

    . . .

   **B** Well, we're *quite* brown . . .

## 5

1 T.13.5.A.

| | |
|---|---|
| technical | official |
| personal | fundamental |
| technological | total |
| legal | global |

*-al* is pronounced / əl /.
*-cial* is pronounced / ʃl /.

2 T.13.5.B.

| | |
|---|---|
| financial | practical |
| social | political |
| national | sexual |
| commercial | theoretical |
| natural | |

3 T.13.5.C.

a. Sorry but it's *totally* impossible.
b. He's working there *illegally*.
c. Well, *theoretically* we can do it.
d. I'm *actually* just going home.
e. Things have changed a lot *politically*.
f. I agree with you, *naturally*.
g. They have *fundamentally* different opinions.
h. He's *internationally* famous.

*-ally* is pronounced / əlı /.

5 T.13.5.D.

a. *Personally*, I agree with you.
b. Some people are against vegetarianism, because they think it's *unnatural*.
c. What are you asking is *physically* impossible.
d. He's very intelligent, but unfortunately he's rather *impractical*.
e. The area of eastern England called New Holland has that name because it's *geographically* very similar to Holland.
f. I'll tell you this *unofficially*, but please don't tell anyone that I told you – if you do, I'll be in serious trouble.
g. This is a *national* disaster.

h. Many people believe that there will be serious *ecological* problems in the next century.
i. There are important *regional* differences between the various parts of Spain.
j. He smokes an *occasional* cigar.

## 7

1 T.13.7.

M *What* was the *temperature* in Lisbon yesterday?
W It was 86 *degrees fahrenheit*.
M *What's that* in centigrade?
W It's . . . 30 *degrees centigrade*.

## 8

1 T.13.8.A.

| | |
|---|---|
| Mr | North |
| Mrs | South |
| Miz | East |
| Doctor | West |
| Professor | North |
| Company | South |
| and Company/ | South East |
| and ċo | South West |
| Limited | North East |
| Avenue | North West |
| Road | care of . . . |
| Street | Saint |
| Square | (pronounced /sənt/) |

2 T.13.8.B.

Doctor James Harvey, fifteen Pelham Avenue, South Leaming.

Goodhand and Company Limited, seventy-three Ferriby Street, Saint Albans.

Miz Louise Hammond, care of Northern trading company, three Town Hall Square, Eastford.

Professor Helen Leach, ninety-seven Springfield Road, London SE 21.

Mr and Mrs G Shaw, sixteen Waterford Square, London W1.

# UNIT 14

## 1

1  T.14.1.A.

   a.  Yale ..... jail
   b.  jet ..... yet
   c.  jaw ..... your
   d.  joke ..... yolk
   e.  use ..... juice

3  T.14.1.A.

   a.  In his youth, Jerry Josephs,

       the New York millionaire,

       used to play jazz on a huge

       German tuba.

   b.  Julian Jones is jealous of

       Eunice's Jaguar, but Eunice

       Jones is jealous of Jason's

       jacuzzi, and Jason Jones is

       jealous of Julian's yacht.

   c.  That fabulous jade unicorn is

       the most beautiful Japanese

       statue in any European

       museum.

   d.  Journalist Jane Young

       stupidly damaged George

       Joyce's new yellow jeep on

       the edge of the bridge.

## 2

2  T.14.2.

| / e / | / ɪ / |
|---|---|
| Kennedy | visit |
| death | related |
| said | office |
| dead | discovered |

| / i: / | / eɪ / |
|---|---|
| beach | pray |
| recent | naked |
| chief | assassinated |
| immediate | |
| peace | |
| disease | |

| / aɪ / |
|---|
| strike |
| biography |
| described |
| find |
| sign |
| died |
| life |

## 3

T.14.3.

| / ɒ / | / ʌ / |
|---|---|
| common | couple |
| intolerable | husband |
| dishonest | courage |
| | become |
| | front |
| | suffer |

| / ɜ: / | / ɔ: / |
|---|---|
| conservative | divorce |
| circumstances | court |
| personally | important |
| hurt | cause |

| / əʊ / | / aʊ / |
|---|---|
| grown | about |
| home | flowers |
| broken | however |
| emotion | |

## 4

1  T.14.4.

The bitter strike over pay and redundancies has now lasted over eight weeks. Shipbuilders have told their leaders to 'fight to the end' to stop dockyards from closing and two thousand of their men losing their jobs.

2  T.14.4.

   a.  The words that become weak are:
       *the* / ðə /; *and* / ənd /; *has* / həz /; *have* / həv /; *to* / tə /; *from* / frəm /; *of* / əv /.

   b.  and c. Linking as shown above.

4  In the rest of the article the **stress**, **weak forms** and **linking** are as follows:

   Sir Albert Pringle, chairman of /əv/ British Shipbuilders, has asked /həz/ Peter Arkwright, the president /ðə/ of the Shipbuilders' Union, to /əvðə/ attend a meeting next Thursday. /ə/ /w/ Meanwhile, the Government has /ðə/ /həz/ ordered Sir Albert to give /tə/ important naval contracts to the /təðə/ Japanese.

## 5

1  T.14.5.A.

The man does not believe what Sally said.

111

To show this there is an **extra** strong stress (nucleus) on *said*.

The intonation **falls** sharply (high fall).

Where's Sally today?
She said she had a headache.
· · ·
Why isn't Sally here today?
She said she had a headache.*

3 | T.14.5.B. |

a. –     e. –
b. *     f. *
c. *     g. –
d. –     h. *

## 6

1 | T.14.6. |

a. i. The first woman is interested.
   ii. The second man is **not** very interested.
b. i. I really thought it **was** funny.
   ii. But it **wasn't very** funny.
c. i. The first man **does** enjoy cooking.
   ii. The second man does **not** enjoy cooking very much.
d. i. The speaker is **not** sure and is really asking a question.
   ii. The speaker **is** sure that this is true and is just checking.
e. i. The woman is just reporting what her husband said – it is neutral.
   ii. The woman does not really believe what her husband said.

## 7

1,2 | T.14.7. |

anger        sarcasm
angry        sarcastic
angrily      sarcastically

pride        shyness
proud        shy
proudly      shyly

tact         cheerfulness
tactful      cheerful
tactfully    cheerfully

apology      generosity
apologetic   generous
apologetically generously

hesitation   stupidity
hesitating   stupid
hesitatingly stupidly

wit          politeness
witty        polite
wittily      politely

3 The following nouns and adjectives have different stress patterns:

sarcasm      sarcastic

apology      apologetic

hesitation   hesitant

generosity   generous

stupidity    stupid

## 8

1 | T.14.8. |

| a. | b. |
| --- | --- |
| organization | famous |
| pronunciation | disastrous |
| description | hilarious |
| explanation | ambitious |

| c. | d. |
| --- | --- |
| frightened | cleverness |
| terrified | meanness |
| fascinated | neatness |
| tired | politeness |

| e. | f. |
| --- | --- |
| revision | careless |
| decision | priceless |
| invasion | useless |
| explosion | worthless |

| g. | h. |
| --- | --- |
| boiling | reasonable |
| freezing | enjoyable |
| disgusting | believable |
| worrying | profitable |

## 9

1 | T.14.9. |

| | |
| --- | --- |
| a. London | l. W1 |
| b. BMW | m. 40 foot |
| c. MOT | n. 16 foot |
| d. A1 | o. £420,000 |
| e. £2,000 | p. £20 |
| f. 500 2276 | q. Mister/Mr |
| g. 6 pm | r. Road |
| h. 350,000 | s. SW3 |
| i. £15 | t. 10 am |
| j. 3 cm | u. 6.30pm |
| k. £30 + VAT | v. 3rd of July |

| T.14.9. |

A London Classified. Can I help you?
B Hello. Yes, I'd like to put an ad in your For Sale section.
A What's the wording?
B BMW for sale. F registration. MOT and taxed. A1 condition. £12,000 or nearest offer. Ring 500 2276 after 6 pm.
C Reach 350,000 Londoners every week. Sell your house or flat in Time Out. 20 words for £15, or a 3 cm box for £30 + VAT.
D I say, this looks nice.
E Oh yes?
D London W1. Spacious sunny top floor flat. 40ft by 16ft. 3 bedrooms and kitchen/diner.
E Mmmm.
D Oh, but it's £420,000. That's rather a lot, isn't it?
F Fancy a pair of Ray-Ban sunglasses for just £20? Come to the Mr Fashion sale at 259 King's Rd. London SW3. Open Monday to Saturday 10 am to 6.30pm. But hurry. Sale ends on the 3rd of July.